TURKMENISCAM

TURKMENISCAM

*How
Washington
Lobbyists
Fought to
Flack for
a Stalinist
Dictatorship*

KEN SILVERSTEIN

RANDOM HOUSE / NEW YORK

Published in the United States by Random House, an imprint of The Random House Publishing Group, a division of Random House, Inc., New York.

RANDOM HOUSE and colophon are registered trademarks of Random House, Inc.

Portions of this work were originally published in *Harper's* in different form.

Library of Congress Cataloging-in-Publication Data
Silverstein, Ken.
Turkmeniscam: how Washington lobbyists fought to flack for a Stalinist dictatorship / Ken Silverstein.
p. cm.
ISBN 978-1-4000-6743-5
1. Lobbying—United States.   2. Pressure groups—United States.
3. Political corruption—United States.   4. United States—Foreign
relations—Turkey.   5. Turkey—Foreign relations—United States.   I. Title.
JK2498.S55 2008
327.730561—dc22   2008008174

Printed in the United States of America on acid-free paper

www.atrandom.com

1 2 3 4 5 6 7 8 9

First Edition

Book design by Susan Turner

TO MY CHILDREN, SOPHIA AND GABRIEL

AUTHOR'S NOTE

My conversations with the lobbyists during our in-person meetings rambled across various topics, as conversations tend to do. In a few instances here, I merged the threads of the conversations.

CONTENTS

PROLOGUE

The Origins of a Journalism Sting

N THE FALL OF 2006, PUBLIC ANGER WAS RUNNING HIGH OVER political scandals involving influence peddler Jack Abramoff and former congressman Randy "Duke" Cunningham—already inmate 94405-198 at the Federal Correctional Institution in Butner, North Carolina, where he was in the midst of serving an eight-year prison term for accepting bribes of cash and hookers from businessmen. As Washington editor of *Harper's* magazine, I was searching for a story that would dramatically expose the power that lobbyists and money continued to wield in the nation's capital, despite exposure of Abramoff, Cunningham, and a host of other Beltway miscreants.

After much pondering, I hit upon an idea that seemed perfect, though a bit unconventional: I would create a phony defense company (peddling a product of dubious utility), retain a well-connected lobbyist, curry favor with a key member of Congress, and seek to win a big fat federal "earmark." The polite term for political pork, earmarks are itemized awards that are quietly attached by members of Congress to the massive bills that fund the federal government. The entire process had become so willfully murky that abuse was no longer the exception but the rule. Indeed, earmarking had been at the heart of several of the recent political scandals. Cunningham, for example, had a bribe menu that spelled out how much money he expected from businessmen for whom he won government awards.

In recent decades, earmarking has become an industry, and many lobby shops specialize in winning them for clients. An especially attractive feature for those private interests seeking earmarks is that they are awarded on a noncompetitive basis and recipients are not required to meet any performance standards. In other words, companies seeking earmarks need not demonstrate that their project or product actually delivers a useful good or service; the key to success is not efficacy but lining up the requisite political support. What better way to demonstrate that Washington was for sale than to win a congressional earmark for my phony firm's phony product with the help of a powerful lobbyist?

First, I had to clear the approach with *Harper's* editor Roger Hodge and senior editor Bill Wasik, who handled my stories. Undercover reporting was long an accepted practice in American journalism, but in recent years it has largely fallen out of favor. The decline can be traced in part to the transformation of journalism from a profession for cynical, underpaid gumshoe reporters into (in Washington at least) a highbrow occupation for opinionmongers, Sunday talk show yakkers, and social climbers. As punditry has replaced muckraking as the profession's highest calling, undercover reporting has been abandoned as too embarrassing and undignified. "No one in a newsroom today would dare sug-

gest that a reporter get information through any kind of sub-
terfuge," William Gaines, who three decades ago worked on undercover assignments for the *Chicago Tribune,* wrote in a 2007
essay titled "The Lost Art of Infiltration." "Such thoughts made
the newspaper's lawyers very nervous in the 1970s, and today I
fear they would respond with derision. Today there is something
called ethics. In Chicago in the 1970s that was thought of as a
poor excuse for not getting the story."

While major American newspapers have dropped undercover reporting, the TV networks and some magazines, *Harper's*
among them, still allow it under some circumstances. In the case
I proposed, I believed the grounds for going undercover were
compelling and clear (more on this in Chapter 7). Hodge and
Wasik agreed and authorized me to proceed, even though they
knew that if and when a story was published, we'd get heat from
some quarters of mainstream journalism for employing undercover tactics.

I warned them as well that there were a number of serious
risks to the project, and no guarantee of success. The lobbyists I
contacted might have moral qualms about seeking money for an
unknown, potentially shady company like the one I envisioned
and decline to take the bait. That, admittedly, was improbable,
but I also had doubts about my ability to convincingly play the
role of a defense contractor, and the whole sting would fizzle if I
aroused the suspicions of the lobbyists I contacted. And even if
we got past that hurdle, I could be busted at any point between
the launch of the plot and publication of the story. For example,
the lobbyists would almost certainly discover something was
amiss if they performed any sort of due diligence background
search on my phony firm, or I might easily blow my cover with
an off-note remark that revealed me as a poser, or some other
amateurish misstep. In a worst-case scenario, a lot of time, plan-

ning, and money of *Harper's* would go down the drain. My editors were prepared to run those risks as well.

Excited by the possibilities, I sketched out a plan. Step one would be to create a fake company, which would have a business address in the Virginia suburbs near Washington, an area that is home to thousands of small defense contractors. I selected for my firm the nondescript name of ACR Engineering, whose initials could stand for either Advanced Communications Research or Astonishing Congressional Rip-off. The latter seemed more apt in this case.

I also needed to come up with a product or concept ACR was seeking to peddle to the Pentagon. One military expert I spoke with said the appropriations process was so crooked that any harebrained scheme would do as long as I retained a lobbyist with the right political connections. "There's a huge pool of money available for defense-related research and development projects," he told me. "Tell your lobbyist you want to outfit a flock of pigeons with cell phones. That will work." This seemed farfetched to me, so I tentatively settled upon a device that was capable of destroying roadside bombs.

Roadside bombs, which had killed so many American soldiers in Iraq and were becoming an increasing threat in Afghanistan, was a genuine priority. In late 2003, the Pentagon established an IED (improvised explosive devices) task force, with a $3 billion budget, that was charged with researching and developing projects to reduce the toll from IEDs used by insurgent groups. With a Pentagon honeypot this size, it was inevitable that a number of companies were seeking to cash in with products of little merit.

Consider here the case of Ionatron, a homeland defense firm with operations in Arizona and Mississippi, created in 2002 out of the shell of a lawn-care company called U.S. Home & Garden

Inc. The founders of Ionatron included Robert Howard, whom the *New York Post* has described as "a twice-fined Wall Street stock promoter . . . who agreed to pay $2.9 million in penalties in 1997 in settlement of a Securities and Exchange Commission suit charging him with making false and misleading statements about another company he founded and controlled." (Howard, who became the company chairman, no longer holds a position with the firm.)

Ionatron's website says it designs and manufactures "directed-energy weapons" that work like "man-made lightning" and are able to "disable people or vehicles that threaten our security." One of the products the firm developed was a lightning bolt to target cars, trucks, and boats; a second system was called "portal denial" (to my ear, that sounds like a fancy name for a door) that is designed to stop intruders "with a lethal or non-lethal electrical discharge"; and a third was its Joint IED Neutralizer (JIN), which was intended to destroy roadside bombs.

In 2003, Ionatron was awarded its first government contract. Curiously, that was the same year that Ionatron retained the services of the Blank Rome lobby shop, whose chairman, David Girard-diCarlo, was a major fund-raiser for President Bush and for Tom Ridge, the former Pennsylvania governor who became the first secretary of the Department of Homeland Security. Blank Rome hired at least two of Ridge's aides to lobby for the firm, and several of its clients have won favors and contracts from DHS. Meanwhile, Ionatron paid Blank Rome hundreds of thousands of dollars in lobbying fees.

Ionatron had also been shelling out for political contributions. Company officials and employees had donated $54,500 to political candidates and committees, with $19,000 of that going to Congressman John Murtha, a Democrat on the Defense Appropriations Subcommittee, and $5,000 for Congressman Hal

Rogers, a Republican who headed the Homeland Security Appropriations Subcommittee.

Since its creation, Ionatron has received tens of millions of dollars in federal money, of which at least $12 million was awarded for its JIN device. A bizarre-looking gadget with what appears to be a giant needle sticking out of its front end, the JIN would supposedly be able to remotely detonate IEDs.

It sounded too good to be true, but in July 2005, Ionatron suggested that the JIN was just about ready to be deployed. Mark Carallo, a company spokesman, made clear that it was patriotism, not profits, that was motivating Ionatron. "There is nothing more terrifying to a soldier than going out on patrol and not knowing what's out there," Carallo said. "This is going to allow our soldiers to have confidence that when they go out on patrol, the threat of IEDs is going to be significantly reduced." (At one PR event, the JIN's exterior was painted in the colors of the American flag.)

Later that year, Ionatron CEO Thomas Dearmin said that the JIN had "exceeded expectations" during testing and that the Pentagon had "determined the units have military utility." The military was so excited, he said, that it was asking "for pricing proposals for JIN production quantities of 50, 500, 1,000 and 2,000 units."

Meanwhile, the media had a brief but passionate love affair with the JIN as well. In mid-2005, *USA Today,* NBC News, and Fox News all did puff pieces on the product. In February 2006, the *Los Angeles Times* asserted that a JIN prototype had "destroyed about 90% of the IEDs laid in its path during a battery of tests" but had not yet been sent into battle, "prompting charges that Pentagon bureaucracy is slowing the effort to protect American troops in Iraq." (In a rare skeptical look, *The Washington Post* in 2005 noted that Ionatron faced an old problem in seeking to utilize lightning as a weapon: "It is notoriously difficult to control. Making it go straight and far requires breaking down the air, like drilling a path through wood for a nail. Creating this path for any more than a few feet presents a formidable challenge.")

In fact, the JIN never was dispatched for combat in Iraq and in May 2006, Ionatron announced that the government had determined that the JIN was not combat-ready. Ionatron stock plummeted more than 39 percent over the next four days, prompting a shareholder suit which claimed that the company's public declarations about the JIN were overly optimistic and that insiders had sold shares worth more than $18 million in the roughly six-month period preceding the stock collapse. By early 2008, at which point Ionatron had changed its name to Applied Energetics, company shares were trading at about two dollars, more than 80 percent off their high.

So for the purposes of my undercover story, I'd say that ACR, my fake firm, had a brilliant idea for an anti-IED device. To get the ball rolling, we needed seed funding from the government through a congressional earmark.

The next step would be to target a lawmaker on one of the congressional appropriations committees—which control the earmarking process—who would be willing, given campaign contributions and other standard blandishments, to seek money for ACR's project. Since the Democrats had won control of both houses of Congress in the November elections, I wanted to select a lawmaker from that party to be ACR's would-be water carrier. Numerous possibilities came to mind. There was Congressman Jim Moran of Virginia, friend to many a small defense contractor and a man who had recently said he planned to "earmark the shit" out of appropriations bills, and the equally alluring Senator Robert Byrd of West Virginia, one of history's most spectacular pork-barrelers. His grandest achievement, perhaps, had been winning a Coast Guard facility for his conspicuously landlocked state. "You may as well slap my wife as take away my transportation funding," Byrd once remarked.

But after further reflection, I concluded that there was really only one man for the job: Congressman Murtha of Pennsylvania, the incoming Democratic chairman of the Defense Appropriations Subcommittee. Hence, all requests for defense earmarks would be vetted by his staff, which would make the ultimate call on which ones would be included in the final defense budget. In addition to being a pork-seeking missile in the Byrd tradition, Murtha has a history of playing it close to the ethical edge. Back in the late 1970s, during the early days of his congressional career, Murtha became embroiled in the ABSCAM sting, during which FBI agents offered various members of Congress bribes in exchange for their granting political favors to Kambir Abdul Rahman, a fictitious Middle Eastern sheikh. One senator and six House members were convicted in the affair; Murtha escaped prosecution but was named as an unindicted co-conspirator, having been videotaped telling an FBI agent that he was not interested "at this point" in taking a fifty-thousand-dollar payoff.

The final step would be picking out a lobbying firm that ACR would retain. Once again, there were a number of strong candidates but also a clear front-runner. When the Republicans ruled Congress, certain lobbying firms and individual lobbyists were known to be especially plugged in with GOP leaders. These included Copeland Lowery Jacquez Denton & White (tight with California congressman Jerry Lewis, head of the House Appropriations Committee), the Alexander Strategy Group (buddies with Tom DeLay), and, of course, Jack Abramoff. With Democrats back in charge, there were new lobbying kings in town. Among the best connected was the PMA Group, which describes

itself on its website as "the premier Washington consulting organization in the defense arena."

PMA was founded in 1989 by Paul Magliocchetti, an ex-
staffer on the House Defense Appropriations Subcommittee,
where he had "responsibility for $30 billion in Navy procure-
ment accounts" (as described in a past PMA pitch to a potential
client that I obtained). PMA has dozens of lobbyists, virtually all
of who came to the firm from Capitol Hill or the Pentagon. PMA,
according to the pitch, "becomes part of your organization and
complements your existing resources." The firm maintains "active liaison with key members of Congress and their staff to safe-
guard client interests," and helps "design and tailor procurement
strategies that maximize successful pursuit of government contract opportunities."

PMA has plenty of powerful friends in Congress, but none
more intimate than Murtha. Its lobbyists include Julie Giardina,
a former Murtha staffer, and Daniel Cunningham, who formerly
worked for the Army and who, Hill sources told me, was extremely close to the congressman. The two are golfing buddies,
and Murtha was said to use Cunningham as his unofficial driver.

There was no doubt about PMA's earmarking firepower. In
2006, according to *The Wall Street Journal*, Murtha received
more than $300,000 in contributions from Magliocchetti and his
clients, who in turn won government contracts worth $95 mil-
lion. Among his blue-chip roster: Lockheed Martin, General Dynamics, Boeing, and CACI International.

A source provided me with a copy of an invitation to a
Murtha fund-raiser that was held on May 10, 2006—exactly two
weeks before the House version of the Pentagon bill was final-
ized. The event, held at the Ritz-Carlton hotel at the Pentagon
City mall in Arlington, Virginia, had the cute name of "Breakfast
for a Champion." It honored Murtha's "Lifetime of Major-League

Service to Country," though clearly it would have been far more accurate to substitute "Industry" for the latter word.

The 102-member host committee for the fund-raiser was comprised almost entirely of defense lobbyists and top officials from military firms. The suggested price of admission to the event: $2,500 for Political Action Committees and $1,000 for individuals. That's a bargain, if you're selling weapons systems worth millions, or even billions, of dollars to the federal government. Particularly conspicuous on the host committee were four lobbyists from the PMA Group, including Magliocchetti and Cunningham. Four PMA Group clients were also listed as members of the committee: Mark Newman, CEO of DRS Technologies; Jay Reddy, founder of ProLogic; Brian Boyle, vice president of Advanced Acoustic Concepts; and Dan DeVos, president of Concurrent Technologies Corporation. The latter's firm was founded with earmarks arranged with Murtha's help and has continued to thrive on federal money funneled to it with the help of the congressman.

Following the Breakfast for a Champion, I learned, after completing more research, that all the firms and lobbyists mentioned above (and plenty of others from the host committee) had received big bucks from Murtha's subcommittee. DRS Technologies alone won at least $6 million from four separate earmarks.

I'm confident that my plan to win an earmark for ACR had a high chance of success, but in the end I had to abandon the idea. First, there were the cruel economic realities. Hiring PMA could cost six thousand a month or more, and earmarking specialists I consulted told me that while they had little doubt that I'd ultimately win congressional funding, it might take more than a year to do so. Hence, I'd need to raise roughly a hundred thousand dollars just to pay PMA's bills. Second, I never intended to actually take possession of the earmarked money—the idea would be to bail out after PMA had persuaded Murtha to insert funding in the defense budget—but deceitfully seeking money for a genuinely important cause raised ethical issues and there were some fairly serious legal issues involved as well. I'd have a great story, but I might end up as Duke Cunningham's cellmate at Victorville.

I was close to abandoning the route of an undercover sting when I hit upon a cheaper but still intriguing idea that would accomplish the same goal of exposing lobbyists' influence. Rather than look for a federal handout, I'd approach a number of top Beltway firms that lobby for foreign interests and see if they'd be interested in representing a government known for its dictatorial ways, human rights abuses, and corruption. I would pose as the representative of a small, mysterious overseas firm with a major financial stake in the country in question, and which hoped to curry favor with the ruling authorities by retaining a Washington firm to buff their image and improve the regime's ties with the American government. I wouldn't need much money, because I wouldn't actually hire a lobbying firm. Instead, I'd have the lobbyists lay out their game plans over the phone and, with luck, during in-person meetings I'd try to set up at their offices.

My editors at *Harper's* agreed that this approach could yield a powerful tale. Hence, I began making preparations for a story that would seek to answer a series of questions: If presented with a potentially fat contract to represent a pariah regime, just how low would a well-heeled Washington lobbying firm sink? Exactly what sorts of promises do these firms make to foreign governments? What kind of scrutiny, if any, do they apply to potential clients? How do they orchestrate support for their clients? And how much of their work would be visible to Congress and the public, and hence subject to scrutiny and debate?

TURKMENISCAM

ONE

A Short History of Foreign Lobbying

W HEN SECRETARY OF STATE CONDOLEEZZA RICE ANNOUNCED the publication of the U.S. government's annual survey of global human rights in March 2007, she said its release demonstrated America's commitment to civil liberties, the rule of law, a free press, and security forces that protect their people instead of repressing them. "We are recommitting ourselves to stand with those courageous men and women who struggle for their freedom and their rights," she stated. "And we are recommitting ourselves to call every government to account that still treats the basic rights of its citizens as options rather than, in President Bush's words, the non-negotiable demands of human dignity."

Yet when one flips through the pages of the report it quickly becomes apparent that many of the countries most severely crit-

icized for human rights abuses had won from the Bush administration foreign aid, military assistance, and expanded trade opportunities. A number of leaders from these countries have also
won coveted White House visits, and accompanying photo ops
with Bush or other senior officials. The aura of legitimacy thus
conferred can help ease doubts among American companies
about investing in their homelands, as well as blunt criticism
from domestic foes.

The granting of favorable concessions to dictatorial regimes is
not a practice limited to the Bush administration, nor is it one re-
stricted to Republican presidents. Bill Clinton came into office
having said that China's access to American markets should be
tied to improved human rights—specifically its willingness to
"recognize the legitimacy of those kids that were carrying the
Statue of Liberty" at Tiananmen Square—and left having granted
Beijing its long-cherished goal of Most Favored Nation (now called
Permanent Normal Trade Relations) status. Jimmy Carter put the
promotion of human rights at the heart of his foreign policy, yet
he cut deals for South American generals and Persian Gulf mon-
archs in much the same fashion as his successor, Ronald Reagan.

How is it that year in and year out, come Republican or
Democratic administration, the world's worst regimes win favors in Washington? In part, because they often have something
highly desired by the United States that can be leveraged to their
advantage, be it oil (e.g., Saudi Arabia), vast markets for trade
and investment (China), or geostrategic importance (Egypt). But
even the most inherently well-endowed regimes need help gam-
ing the Washington system, and it is their great fortune that
countless lobbyists are, for the right price, invariably willing to
lend a hand.

Lobbyists have been aiding and abetting pariah regimes
since at least as far back as the 1930s, when the Nazi govern-

ment, through a firm called the German Dye Trust, retained Ivy Lee, the father of modern public relations, to favorably influence American public opinion of the Third Reich.

Lee's most famous domestic client was John D. Rockefeller, the industrialist and founder of Standard Oil who became the world's richest man. Under Lee's guidance, *Time* magazine reported in 1934 (in an article about Lee's work for the Nazis), Rockefeller "was metamorphosed from a corporate monster into a benevolent old philanthropist." Lee's PR work for Rockefeller included sanitizing the Ludlow Massacre of 1914, when the Colorado National Guard killed dozens of people, among them women and children, during attacks on striking coal miners and their families at Ludlow, Colorado. The strikers worked for the Rockefeller-family-owned Colorado Fuel & Iron Company and two other mining companies; Lee falsely claimed that some of the victims of the Guard, which effectively worked at the behest of the Rockefellers, had died of smoke inhalation from an overturned stove. He also spread word that the famous labor leader Mother Jones, who supported the strikers, ran a whorehouse. Lee's work at Ludlow earned him the moniker "Poison Ivy" from the writer Upton Sinclair.

Lee, who was paid $25,000 per year for his efforts in Germany, plotted a campaign that included influencing American views with pro-Hitler newspaper pieces and radio addresses. He proposed that the Nazi government's plans for a military buildup be portrayed as central to "preventing for all time the return of the Communist peril." In its 1934 story, *Time* derided the distinction Lee had recently sought to draw between the Dye Trust and the Nazi regime during an appearance before a congressional committee. "Inasmuch as [the Dye Trust] was one of the two early and potent backers of Adolf Hitler and inasmuch as the German Government has assumed pretty thorough control of private business, the committee got the impression that Mr. Lee might just as well have been retained by the Reichskanzler himself," the magazine said.

Exposure of Lee's deal led Congress to pass the Foreign Agents Registration Act (FARA), which required foreign lobbyists to register their contracts with the Justice Department. The idea seemed to be that with the need for disclosure, lobbyists would find it too embarrassing to take on clients that were hideously immoral or corrupt, no matter how much money they were offered. That assumption proved to be naïve. The FARA may have temporarily dissuaded American flacks from signing up monstrous clients, but before long it was business as usual. Latin American military men, corrupt Middle Eastern sheikhs, murderous generals from Africa and Asia—they've all come looking for help in Washington, D.C., over the years, and they have rarely returned home disappointed.

The Reagan years were a particularly rich period for foreign lobbyists, as the president backed a host of anticommunist "freedom fighters" around the globe with military and political support. The problem was that these freedom fighters—from Afghanistan to Angola to Nicaragua—were rape-and-pillage artists who regularly committed atrocities against civilians during their campaigns. Hence, dressing them up as the moral equivalent of "America's founding fathers," as Reagan famously described the "contra" rebels in Nicaragua, was required in order to persuade the American public and Congress that these groups were worthy of support. Beltway lobbyists eagerly rose to the challenge.

One remarkable piece of lobbyist image management was carried out by the firm of Black, Manafort, Stone and Kelly, which helped refashion the public profile of Jonas Savimbi, a murderous, demented Angolan rebel leader backed by the apartheid regime in South Africa. Savimbi visited Washington on numerous occasions, where the lobby shop had him ferried about by stretch limousine to meetings with political leaders, think tanks, and TV networks. Black, Manafort checked repeated threats by members of Congress to cut off aid to Savimbi's rebel group, which plundered its way through Angola with the help of billions in aid from American taxpayers.

In 1992, the now defunct *Spy* magazine ran a feature on foreign lobbyists titled "Publicists of the Damned," which chronicled the activities of a veritable rogues' gallery of foreign lobbyists. There was Joseph Blatchford, who ran the Peace Corps during the Nixon administration but then promoted the right-wing regime of Alfredo "Freddy" Cristiani, president of El Salvador. "All we heard over and over was that he [Cristiani] was a puppet of the death squads, a creature of millionaire coffee growers," Blatchford complained to *Spy*. As the magazine drolly noted, "That unfortunate reputation is due in part to the fact that Cristiani was the candidate of the right-wing ARENA party, which was founded by death squad mastermind Roberto D'Aubuisson and supported by millionaire coffee growers."

Tom Scanlon, a lobbyist for the Dominican Republic, had the difficult task of defending his client against charges of using children as slave laborers in sugar fields. What made the job especially aggravating was that the charges had been amply documented by an ABC News report. Asked about the clear presence in the ABC videos of young cane cutters, Scanlon said, "[The adult workers] just like to bring their children with them to help out in the fields." *Spy* found Tommy Boggs, long one of the most influential lobbyists in town, seeking to ease foreign aid restrictions on the government of Guatemala, which was engaged in a murderous campaign to stamp out political opposition.

"What's your problem?" Boggs asked a congressional staffer

whom he failed to sway about Guatemala's commitment to reform, according to *Spy*.

"These guys are murderers and thugs," the aide said forthrightly of Boggs's client.

"What would convince you that they're moving in the right direction?" Boggs asked eagerly.

"I'd be impressed if they undertook a land reform program," the aide told him.

Upon which Boggs replied: "You want a land reform program? I can have a land reform program on your desk this afternoon."

Spy contacted a number of top Washington lobbying firms seeking representation for the German People's Alliance, a bogus neo-Nazi group invented by the magazine. The Alliance's representative—"Sabina Hofer," who was actually a *Spy* office worker from Germany and hence had the appropriate accent—told the lobbyists that her group was headquartered in Bremerhaven, then a hotbed of radical right-wing activity. The Alliance's goals included ridding Germany of immigrants, increasing its voice in the U.S. Congress to counter the pro-Jewish claque, and "reclaiming" Poland.

This proved to be too much to stomach even for most of the lobbyists contacted by *Spy*. Stu Sweet of Black, Manafort, Stone and Kelly—not, as we just saw, a firm known for squeamishness about representing malodorous clients—took offense when Hofer mentioned a software program designed by German and Austrian programmers that allowed players to run their own concentration camps. She said a controversy that had erupted about the software was silly and said the whole thing was nothing more than "children playing." Sweet replied: "How would the German people feel if there were American companies that had computer games that said, 'Kill as many Germans as possible'?"

But there was one lobbyist that Hofer called who aggressively tried to land the contract: Edward J. von Kloberg III. Upon hearing that the group had up to a million dollars to spend, von Kloberg breathlessly told Hofer, "I believe in many of the tenets that you believe in. So we are not very far apart, my dear."

At the time, David Duke was a noxious figure on the national political stage. A founder of the Knights of the Ku Klux Klan and the National Association for the Advancement of White People, he won a House seat in the Louisiana state legislature in 1989. In currying favor with Hofer, von Kloberg suggested that Duke's popularity indicated potential American support for the Alliance's own goals, and told her that realization of her group's aims was "entirely possible."

Von Kloberg's eagerness to strike a deal with Hofer wasn't wholly surprising. Now deceased, he for years made quite a comfortable living by representing some of the world's vilest regimes. In the 1980s he was hired by Saddam Hussein of Iraq, and earned his keep by justifying that government's gassing of its Kurdish population. He also represented Mobutu Sese Seko of Zaire, who in stealing billions from his national treasury racked up one of the most brazen and spectacular records of political corruption in modern history. Von Kloberg helped win American foreign aid for Mobutu, and when his client was ousted by a rebel army, he promptly went to work for Laurent Kabila, the murderous warlord who overthrew him. Two other von Kloberg contracts—for Nicolae Ceauşescu of Romania and Samuel Doe of Liberia—were terminated, quite literally, when their own citizens murdered them. Von Kloberg publicly regretted working for only one client, the Burmese government, and that wasn't because of its brutal human rights record but because it stiffed him for thousands of dollars in fees.

Von Kloberg was a scam artist in his private life as well. Even his name was fake: he inserted "von" because he thought it made him sound like European nobility. More seriously, he was convicted in 1984 of a felony for forging bogus contracts with foreign governments, which he used in seeking a $60,000 bank loan.

Yet nothing he said or did ever hurt von Kloberg's reputation in Washington, not his criminal record, nor his attempt to land a neo-Nazi group as a client, nor his kind words for David Duke. After the *Spy* article ran, he showed up at the party for the magazine's new Washington office wearing a trench helmet and gas mask. "I can take the flak," he proclaimed. *Washingtonian* magazine soon published a flattering profile of von Kloberg. "One of Washington's true characters," it called him. "He maintains friendly relations with Washington's powerful, and his dinners for legislators and opinion-makers at the Jockey Club are legendary."

Von Kloberg's lobbying work finally came to an end in 2002, due to health problems. Three years later, suffering from cancer and depressed over the end of a romance, he jumped from the Castel Sant'Angelo in Rome. "A few months before von Kloberg leaped from the parapet (with a note for his lover in one pocket and in another a copy of a magazine cover with a photo of him standing next to George H. W. Bush), disgraced superlobbyist Jack Abramoff stood before a congressional committee investigating his ethics and took the Fifth," Art Levine, the author of the *Spy* piece, wrote in an obituary. "Von Kloberg was a stranger to such modesty. He lived without apology and died for love, and in both instances he was increasingly an anachronism in the world he helped create."

Nor were other lobbying firms chastened by von Kloberg's outing. Just as was the case with Ivy Lee's Nazi deal and passage of the FARA, there was hardly a pause for reflection before sleazy new agreements were being concluded.

One particularly nasty example, inked a few years later, was a half-million-dollar agreement between a lobby firm called Jefferson Waterman International (JWI) and Burma's military government. JWI employed many executives who had passed through the Beltway's revolving door. The firm's top two executives were Ann Wrobleski, assistant secretary of state for international narcotics matters in the Reagan and George H. W. Bush administrations, and Charles Waterman, who formerly worked for the CIA's Near East division. With those sorts of contacts, JWI boasted on its website, the firm was "able to obtain early, authoritative information on international policy developments, decisions, and opportunities that can affect a country's or a company's future.... This information—discreetly acquired, expertly analyzed, and reported on a timely basis—lays the groundwork for effective strategies or signals the need for immediate action."

Burma was not your run-of-the-mill dictatorship. Opposition forces led by Nobel Peace Prize winner Aung San Suu Kyi swept national elections in 1990, winning more than 80 percent of the seats in parliament and leading the generals to annul the balloting and rule by terror. "Throughout the tropical nation, world-class drug lords operate a wink's length from the regime and heavily-armed ethnic militias roam wild, spreading narcotics, arms, and instability to neighboring countries," said a story in the *Washington Monthly* at the time.

JWI was understandably embarrassed by handling such an account, so a company called Myanmar Resource Development Ltd. stood in for the junta, playing the role that the German Dye Trust had performed in the Nazi–Ivy Lee deal of 1934. The maneuver fooled no one. State Department memos from the period showed that American officials recognized that JWI was working directly for the junta.

When she worked for Reagan and Bush Senior, Wrobleski had been an outspoken critic of the Burmese government, accusing it of being a leading exporter of heroin to the United States. In 1989 she said that there was little hope that Burma would crack down on drug trafficking "until a government enjoying greater credibility and support among the Burmese people" replaced the military regime.

In handling the Burma account for JWI, Wrobleski helped paint an entirely different picture. One of her tactics was to provide American journalists with all-expense-paid trips to Burma, where they would hear government officials express their supposed commitment to combating drug trafficking. The plan backfired, however, when a *Newsweek* reporter noticed that a quantity of poppy plants destroyed for the benefit of the visiting scribes "had already been drained of opium." The *Newsweek* story also quoted a diplomat as describing Burma as a "haven for retired opium warlords and their money."

JWI also launched an Internet newsletter, the Myanmar Monitor, which was supposed to "provide a broad and balanced view of Burma." This consisted of stories about tourism (visitors, it advised, would encounter a country where "loving kindness, sympathy, tolerance, benevolence, mutual regard, respect, and humanitarianism evolve out of Buddha's teachings") and the junta's fervent belief in political reform. One Monitor commentary hailed the generals for the way they "somehow managed to unify the country, restored social order and brought stability back to the nation."

Back in the real world, developments weren't nearly as promising. Among the developments the Monitor somehow missed during this period were a roundup of opposition activists; the State Department's 1997 "decertification" of Burma, for the seventh consecutive year, as an ally in the war on drugs; and the regime's banishment from a London meeting of European and Asian governments. British foreign secretary Robin Cook explained that Burma was "one of the few governments in the world whose members are prepared to profit out of the drug trade."

Like von Kloberg, JWI decided to sever its ties to the Burmese regime only after the generals—angry that the United States and other Western nations boycotted an international conference on heroin trafficking in Rangoon—stiffed the lobbying firm for its fees.

BEFORE JACK ABRAMOFF BEGAN BUYING CONGRESSMEN AND RIPPING off Native American tribes, he, too, performed public relations work for Reagan's freedom fighters (albeit of a decidedly more covert nature than Black, Manafort's job for Savimbi). As chairman of the College Republican National Committee, Abramoff visited South Africa in 1983. Three years later, he became the first chairman of the International Freedom Foundation (IFF)—a seemingly independent right-wing group headquartered in Washington, D.C., that was run by South African intelligence under the code name of Pacman. "The South Africans needed front men," a source that worked closely with the IFF told me. "Abramoff was identified early on as an ambitious, up-and-coming American conservative who could be useful." Abramoff, he said, was a willing asset of the apartheid government.

The IFF advocated for the contras in Nicaragua and the mujahideen rebels in Afghanistan, but its primary interest was South Africa. Much of the group's energy was spent attempting to discredit Nelson Mandela and the global antiapartheid movement, opposing sanctions on the South African government, and building support for Jonas Savimbi, who was strongly backed by Pretoria as well as Washington.

Abramoff ran the IFF until 1989, the year he produced *Red Scorpion*, an anticommunist parable filmed in Namibia that co-starred muscle-bound Dolph Lundgren as a Savimbi-like rebel leader and the singer Grace Jones as his sidekick. Abramoff always described *Red Scorpion* as strictly a show business venture, but it was later revealed to be a project of the IFF and South African military intelligence.

South Africa pulled the money plug on the IFF in the fall of 1991, and it sputtered on for a few more years before closing up shop. In 1995 *Newsday* disclosed that the group had been a South African government project. Additional details emerged in reports from South Africa's Truth and Reconciliation Commission: while the IFF did generate a small part of its own income through fund-raising, that was primarily to provide cover for the as much as $1.5 million per year the group received from the apartheid government.

Front groups, cutouts, bogus charities, financial trickery, and double-budgeted projects—all the tricks Abramoff later refined when he worked the Beltway lobby trade—seem to have originated with his friends at South African intelligence. Edwin Buckham, Tom DeLay's former chief of staff and pastor, worked closely with Abramoff during his lobbying glory days. Buckham ran the tax-exempt U.S. Family Network, which received millions of dollars from Abramoff's clients, a good part of which reportedly ended up in the pockets of Buckham and his wife.

Michael Scanlon, Abramoff's chief partner in crime, organized a think tank called the American International Center that was headquartered in a $4.2 million house in Rehoboth Beach, Delaware, just blocks off the ocean. The center's purpose, according to an article in *The Weekly Standard,* was "enhancing the methods of empowerment for territories, commonwealths, and sovereign nations in possession of and within the United States" and to "expand the parameters of international discourse in an effort to leverage the combined power of world intellect." Two "resident scholars" lived in the house/headquarters: David Grosh, Rehoboth's 1995 "lifeguard of the year," and Brian Mann, a former yoga instructor.

Abramoff's antics were extreme, but lobbyists routinely practice deception and trickery in the course of their work. Given the product being pushed, that's a virtual necessity for foreign lobbyists with dodgy clients. For example, in 2004 the firm of Patton Boggs registered to represent the government of Cameroon and was paid $99,972 that year to advise the government "on a variety of public policy issues." That latter clause apparently covered helping President Paul Biya, who has ruled since 1982, to pretty up a rigged election in which he won with 71 percent of the vote.

Patton Boggs arranged for six former members of the American Congress to serve as allegedly independent "observers" for the election, which was held in October 2004. The Biya government paid all expenses of the observers, whose trip and agenda was arranged by Patton Boggs lobbyist Greg Laughlin, himself a former member of Congress. International monitors led by a former Canadian prime minister were critical of the balloting, and Roman Catholic cardinal Christian Tumi of Cameroon said the election was "surrounded by fraud."

But the Patton Boggs team was far more upbeat. Even as the votes were being counted, Laughlin—who was not an official member of the delegation, but was identified in Cameroonian and foreign news accounts as its leader—praised the transparency of the vote, with media accounts quoting him as saying, "The elections were conducted fairly." One American observer, former Mississippi congressman Ronnie Shows, told local reporters, "In general, the process was free. This is what democracy is about."

Other delegation members made similar comments, which were given wide coverage by Cameroon's pro-government media outlets. "Voting Conduct Impresses American Observers," ran a headline in a state-owned newspaper. According to the article, the Americans had "exalted" the country's democratic process. It quoted an unidentified team member saying, "Cameroon is well on its way in the democratic process." The British Broadcasting Corp. and the Agence France-Presse news agency reported that former members of Congress had backed up the Biya government's denials of election fraud.

The American team issued a report a week after the vote that was more critical than the comments the delegation members had made in Cameroon. But it concluded that the irregularities were not enough to "disapprove of the balloting process itself" and spoke of "an important degree of progress against the background of past elections." It was just the sort of handout that Patton Boggs's lobbyists could make use of on Capitol Hill. Former congressman Richard Schulze, one of the six election "observers" on the team, also got good mileage from the report. Just a month after the election, he signed up a new client for his lobbying firm: the Biya government. In exchange for an initial retainer of $149,972, he and two other lobbyists at Valis Associates would help "maximize the impact of Cameroon's political and economic reforms on agencies and departments of the U.S. government."

In the case of Cameroon, Patton Boggs sent an allegedly independent bunch of do-gooders to help sell the regime. In a 2007 case, a lobbying firm called Bob Lawrence & Associates brought a group of supposed Azeri humanitarians to Washington for similar purposes. The lobby shop set up an event at the National Press Club in Washington that featured a delegation from the Association for Civil Society Development in Azerbaijan

(ACSDA). "We are coming to...share our experiences in an emerging democracy that is not even a generation old," the delegation leader, ACSDA vice president Vali Alibayov, stated in a press release. His organization's aim, he said, was to "contribute to the development of civil society in Azerbaijan." Patrice Courtney of Bob Lawrence & Associates, who accompanied the delegation in Washington, described the ACSDA as a group that operated independently of the government and called its members notable "scholars and intellectuals."

In reality, the whole affair was a government propaganda mission, and delegation members were hardly as exalted a bunch as Courtney claimed. Bob Lawrence & Associates turned out to be on the payroll of Renaissance Associates, a pro-government business group based in Baku, the Azeri capital, that promoted the interests of President Ilham Aliyev. The president had inherited power from his father—described by diacritica.com, a website that covered post-Soviet affairs in Eastern Europe, as a "protege of...KGB henchmen like Yuri Andropov," and as a man who "stabbed, stole and strong-armed his way to power"—upon the latter's death in 2002 and then won election in a rigged vote the following year.

The ACSDA's activities include election monitoring and polling. In one survey it conducted, according to a *New Republic* story, the ACSDA found that many Azeris believed there was no corruption in Azerbaijan, even though Transparency International has consistently rated it as one of the most corrupt countries in the world. The group's exit polls for 2004 municipal elections found that 99.85 percent of voters felt no pressure while voting. Yet, as *The New Republic* noted, a U.S. government agency sponsored its own poll and found that the municipal elections were even more fraudulent than the presidential election held the year before, which had been universally condemned. And the magazine quoted an international observer who monitored the elections as saying that he didn't recall seeing anyone from the group actually conducting surveys at polling stations and believed the ACSDA just made its numbers up.

Peter Zalmayev, who formerly was a program manager at the International League for Human Rights and who has worked closely with major independent Azeri social and political groups, described the ACSDA to me as "a front operation that helps the government counter criticism from legitimate nongovernmental organizations." He said that many of its member groups were simply shell organizations, in some cases just one-man operations.

Consider the Caspian Partnership for the Future One, one of the ACSDA's member groups. Rustam Mammadov, the group's head, worked from 1997 to 2004 as the head of a section at the "Apparatus of the President of the Azerbaijan Republic, Social-Political Relations Department," according to his biography. Then there's a member group called Human Rights in the XXI Century, which argues, in a throwback to the Soviet era, that there are no political prisoners in Azerbaijan and state repression is a myth. Outsiders believe that Azeri government authorities lock up their foes and generally conduct "uncivilized struggle against its political opponents," but that's merely propaganda from "leading figures of the parties which are in the opposition to the present government."

THERE'S A COMMON PERCEPTION THAT LOBBYISTS ARE ABLE, THROUGH contacts, campaign contributions, and arm-twisting, to win any goal they wish for their clients. (That perception is quite useful to lobbyists in their efforts to woo and land new business.) There are, however, distinct limits to what they can generally achieve.

"Hiring a lobbyist gains foreign governments entry into the Washington political world; it's like the secret handshake that gets you into the lodge," one former lobbyist told me. "But it's hard to actually accomplish anything unless there is already political support for your cause." JWI, for example, never managed to do much good for Burma, probably because its client had no great military or strategic value to the United States and there was relatively limited American corporate investment or interest in the country.

But lobbyists can be highly effective in solidifying and enhancing their clients' ambitions when they have the right raw materials. Energy reserves can work wonders in winning countries a moral blank check, as seen in the case of Saudi Arabia. "If the Saudis grew artichokes we wouldn't care about the relationship, but we want their oil," Lawrence Korb, assistant secretary of defense during the Reagan years, once told me. "That's why we put up with a lot from the Saudis and rarely lean on them."

Dictators sitting atop energy reserves have found an especially receptive ear under the Bush/Cheney administration, in which the president, vice president, and numerous other top officials are former oilmen. Securing foreign sources of energy has been an administration priority since its earliest days. Back in March 2001, just two months after Bush took office, Energy Secretary Spencer Abraham was warning that the United States faced a major energy supply crisis over the next two decades. Two months later, a Cheney-led energy task force issued a report—prepared with the assistance of numerous industry executives and lobbyists who were invited to help out—that urged that the United States find sources of imports other than the Organization of the Petroleum Exporting Countries, citing especially the Caspian region and sub-Saharan Africa. The task force downplayed conservation as a means of reducing the gap between domestic production and demand. "Conservation may be a sign of personal virtue, but it is not a sufficient basis for a sound, comprehensive energy policy," Cheney said.

The goal of moving the United States away from dependence on Middle Eastern oil gained steam after the September 11 attacks. Meanwhile, the administration stated it would no longer ignore human rights violations in the Arab world as a means of ensuring access to energy resources. In a November 2003 speech at the Washington headquarters of the U.S. Chamber of Commerce, nine months after the invasion of Iraq, President Bush sharply denounced not just tyranny in the Arab states but the logic by which the West had abetted it. "Western nations excusing and accommodating the lack of freedom in the Middle East did nothing to make us safe—because in the long run, stability cannot be purchased at the expense of liberty," he said. "As long as the Middle East remains a place where freedom does not flourish, it will remain a place of stagnation, resentment, and violence ready for export." Saying it would be "reckless to accept the status quo," Bush called for a new "forward strategy of freedom in the Middle East." At least in its rhetoric, this was nothing less than a blanket repudiation of six decades of American foreign policy.

In the end, the Bush administration proved quite content to accommodate the lack of freedom in countries ruled by America's Middle East allies. For example, King Abdullah of Saudi Arabia continued to arrest government critics and rejected calls to hold elections for even a toothless "consultative council." Yet other than a few empty rhetorical flourishes from American officials criticizing its lack of democracy, Saudi Arabia suffered no significant fallout for flouting what American pundits referred to as Bush's "freedom agenda."

In response to Arab anger over U.S. support for Israel and

the invasion of Iraq, the administration heightened its drive to forge closer ties with oil-rich regimes outside the Persian Gulf. But the new suppliers the United States turned to have plenty of unappealing features of their own. The collapse of the Soviet Union opened the door to large reserves in the Caspian Basin, but the countries of the region are headed by authoritarian regimes that tolerate little political opposition. Improved technology has increased oil production in sub-Saharan Africa, but the boom there has bred massive government corruption. "Global oil is a mixed picture, predominantly negative, and African oil is the most negative of all the stories," David Gordon, head of the CIA's Office of Transnational Issues, said at an energy conference I attended a few years ago. Gordon, who had recently traveled to Nigeria, said that the consensus among people he spoke with was that the country would have been better off if its oil had been left in the ground. That's a reasonable conclusion when one considers that Nigeria has exported more than $200 billion worth of oil during the last few decades but the overwhelming majority of its people live in poverty.

Traditionally, human rights concerns just didn't count for much when the United States went looking for overseas oil, and they counted for even less after 9/11. Although America's new oil allies "are often a threat to their own people . . . they do not harbor or finance groups that threaten U.S. interests," David Goldwyn, a former Energy Department official and oil industry consultant, told Congress in 2002. In other words, it's okay if foreign dictators kill their own people just as long as they don't kill us (and continue to sell us their oil).

Oil combined with geostrategic importance is a particularly winning combination for dictators and the lobbyists they hire. Saudi Arabia, again, is Exhibit A, but consider here the lesser-known example of Kazakhstan. In 2004, President Bush issued a presidential proclamation barring corrupt foreign officials from entering the United States. Yet just two years later, Kazakh president Nursultan Nazarbayev, who has ruled his country since it won independence from the Soviet Union in 1991, came to town for an official visit and received the red carpet treatment, including a meeting with Bush. (The Kazakh leader also flew to Maine, where he dropped in at the Bush family compound in Kennebunkport.)

It's hard to see how Nazarbayev's visit could possibly be squared with Bush's anticorruption proclamation. As of this writing, James Giffen, an American business consultant, was set to be tried in the Southern District Court of New York on charges that he funneled more than $78 million in bribes to Nazarbayev and his former prime minister. The U.S. government's indictment says the bribe money came from fees Giffen received from American oil companies that won stakes in Kazakhstan's oil fields. In addition to showering Nazarbayev with cash, Giffen allegedly bought his-and-her snowmobiles for the president and his wife, bought a fur coat for Mrs. Nazarbayev, and paid the tuition at George Washington University for the president's daughter.

Nazarbayev's record on human rights makes him equally embarrassing as a White House guest. He has a long record of crushing opposition parties and shutting down critical media outlets. A number of government foes have met mysterious and untimely deaths as well. One critic, Zamanbek Nurkadilov, was found dead in his home. The Kazakh government claimed that he killed himself, and from appearances, he was a man determined to end his life: the official story is he shot himself three times, twice in the chest and once in the head. It wasn't explained whether Nurkadilov shot himself in the head before firing into his chest, or vice versa.

Oil is one reason that Nazarbayev gets a free pass. Along

with Azerbaijan, Kazakhstan is a major Caspian energy producer, and American companies, led by Chevron, have invested billions there. Furthermore, close ties to Kazakhstan have been deemed important to national security. Nazarbayev allowed U.S. warplanes to use the airport in Almaty, Kazakhstan's largest city, during the invasion of Afghanistan, and he has been a close ally in the Bush administration's "war on terror" ever since.

Kazakhstan also counts on support from powerful American friends such as James A. Baker III, who served as secretary of state under George Bush père and who was dispatched to Florida to coordinate the Bush-Cheney campaign's recount effort in the state during the disputed 2000 election. Baker had brokered the emerging U.S.-Kazakh relationship during the final days of the Soviet Union. In 1991, he traveled to the country to meet with Nazarbayev, and the two men discussed future bilateral relations while enjoying a sauna at a villa in the mountains above Almaty. Baker is currently at the Houston-based Baker Botts law firm, which advises energy companies seeking to invest in Kazakhstan and other Caspian countries.

Finally, Nazarbayev has spent millions on American lobbyists to help shore up support for his government. The public relations campaign was ginned up in 1998, a year that by most accounts marked a serious downturn in Kazakhstan's human rights situation. Several newspapers that had been critical of the government were shut down. The regime passed a "national security" law that was used widely to deter political opponents. The law, which was enacted as public criticism of Nazarbayev was mounting, defined "unsanctioned gatherings" and "prevention of the growth of investment activity" as threats to the homeland.

Western governments called on Nazarbayev to improve the situation. Instead, with the assistance of American PR specialists, he tried to spin it. Over the next two years, his regime paid more than $4 million to consultants with at least nine public relations companies, law firms, and lobby shops.

It was James Giffen, Nazarbayev's close friend, who led the offensive. A New York business consultant with a law degree from UCLA, Giffen began negotiating deals for American companies in the Soviet Union in the 1980s and met Nazarbayev during the Soviet era. According to the indictment later filed by U.S. prosecutors, the Kazakh leader assigned him to negotiate deals with foreign oil companies seeking to invest in Kazakhstan after the country's independence.

Nazarbayev gave Giffen a Kazakh diplomatic passport and the title of "counselor to the president." When Nazarbayev traveled to the United States, Giffen accompanied him to meetings with government officials. "He was Washington's de facto ambassador to Kazakhstan," Robert Baer, a former CIA officer, told me.

Giffen rounded up some of Washington's top political consultants, who traveled to Almaty to huddle with Nazarbayev in 1998. The mission they returned home with was to convince the world that his oil-rich, authoritarian regime was actually a budding democracy. The team that met in Almaty, dubbed the P-Group (P for political), included James Langdon, Jr., an energy lawyer and leading fund-raiser for George Bush. His firm, Akin Gump Strauss Hauer & Feld (Akin Gump), received a million dollars for its legal and lobbying work on Kazakhstan's behalf.

The three other key P-Group members were Michael Deaver (now deceased), a former deputy chief of staff to President Reagan who was then vice chairman of public relations giant Edelman; Jay Kriegel, a prominent corporate consultant and former senior vice president at CBS Inc. who was charged with keeping Giffen "fully and regularly apprised of activities, intelligence and problems" in the P-Group (according to an internal memo); and Mark Siegel, a former Democratic National Committee executive director, who at the time served on the board of the National Democratic Institute, which was supposed to be promoting democracy programs in Kazakhstan. Siegel's contract called for a daily rate of $2,800 to $3,000 from the Kazakh government.

The P-Group developed a thick strategy document and presented it to Nazarbayev on September 1, 1998. The document said that the P-Group members "strongly believe in democracy"; however, they recognized Kazakhstan's need to "balanc[e] international norms and demands for reform with the need for political stability." Translation: Try your best, but we'll understand if you need to toss a few critics in jail and shut down opposition newspapers.

A month after receiving the document, Nazarbayev called a presidential election for January 10, 1999, nearly two years earlier than planned. Parliament simultaneously passed constitutional amendments that increased the presidential term from five to seven years and abolished a requirement for a 50 percent minimum turnout. Shortly thereafter, Nazarbayev barred his primary opponent from running and subsequently forced him into exile.

Nonetheless, the P-Group sought to ensure, as one confidential document it produced for Kazakh officials put it, that the election would be "perceived by the international community as free and fair." This proved a hard sell when observers broadly condemned the election, in which Nazarbayev won 82 percent of the vote. Before long, the P-Group disbanded, after it was reported that Giffen's activities in Kazakhstan were the target of a federal investigation.

To keep bilateral relations on track, U.S. oil companies with major investments in Kazakhstan stepped up their own efforts.

In 2000, ExxonMobil, ChevronTexaco, and ConocoPhillips helped found and finance the U.S.-Kazakhstan Business Association. The following year, the association and oil company lobbyists helped assemble the Congressional Silk Road Caucus, which fought for closer ties between the United States and Kazakhstan and other Central Asian states. The caucus's co-chairs, Senators Sam Brownback and Mary Landrieu, were among the biggest congressional recipients of campaign contributions from oil and gas interests.

Kazakhstan also supplemented this firepower by hiring several lobbying firms to replace the P-Group. Among them was Patton Boggs, which received $60,000 per month from the Nazarbayev government. In 2002, Texas congressman Joe Barton, chairman of the House Energy and Commerce Committee, inserted a statement in the *Congressional Record* in support of Kazakhstan. "Mr. Speaker, if the United States is to become truly energy independent, it must seek non-OPEC alternatives for our supply of oil," the statement said. "Kazakhstan can—and is willing to—help greatly in this endeavor."

Patton Boggs, it turned out, had drafted the statement for him.

The years of lobbying by and for Kazakhstan paid off. Over the past few years, the U.S. government dropped the country from a list of "non-market economies" that can be hit with particularly tough sanctions in the event of trade disputes with the United States. (The decision came months after a report from the Heritage Foundation, a conservative think tank, ranked Kazakhstan 131st among 161 countries in terms of economic freedom.) Meanwhile, the Bush administration has repeatedly certified (as required by law for foreign aid to flow to Kazakhstan) that the Nazarbayev regime had shown "significant improvement" in human rights, even though no other observers have spotted such improvement. The White House visit of Nazarbayev, a long-cherished goal of his government, was merely the crowning achievement of the lobbying campaign.

There are many other lobbying-for-dictators campaigns that could be cited here, and more still that we surely never hear of, in part because many of those who clearly ought to register as foreign lobbyists don't do so. The U.S. General Accounting Office estimated in 1990 that only about half of all foreign lobbyists properly register, and there is no evidence that matters have notably improved since then. In theory, lobbyists can be heavily fined and even go to prison for violations of the FARA, but there have been only a handful of prosecutions during the act's life. Furthermore, there's so much wiggle room built into the law that even many who aggressively advocate on behalf of foreign governments can argue that they don't fall under FARA's provisions.

For those lobbyists who do register, figuring out what they do on behalf of their clients is extremely difficult because disclosure requirements are so lax. Periodic revelations that do emerge (such as those discussed in this chapter) are generally the result of investigative journalism or, as in the case of James Giffen, criminal investigations. What becomes public is clearly the tip of the iceberg.

So, for example, we know that Turkey has for years spent millions of dollars on lobbyists to fend off a congressional resolution that would label as genocide the Turkish massacre of Armenians during the early twentieth century. With significant help from weapons manufacturers, lobbyists for Saudi Arabia have over the years won congressional support for billions of dollars in arms sales to Riyadh, despite the kingdom's crummy human rights record. Ethiopia's Washington lobbyists in 2007 blocked congressional action that would restrict its foreign aid package—even as Human Rights Watch issued a report saying that the Ethiopian military troops were "destroying villages and property, confiscating livestock, and forcing civilians to relocate" in the course of waging a campaign against a separatist insurgency.

Public disclosure forms list the names—at least some of the names—of the lobbyists who work for these governments, and roughly how much their firms get paid. But what deals they cut and how lobbyists manage to win votes for such inherently unpopular causes are largely unknown, and unknowable under current rules.

TWO

Finding the Right Client:
Make Benefit Glorious Nation of Turkmenistan

WASHINGTON LOBBYISTS ARE NOT GENERALLY DEEMED TO BE a group with high ethical standards, and foreign lobbyists, with their track record of working for Nazis, drug-running despots, and death squad dictators, are widely thought to be the lowest type of Beltway pond scum. In putting together my foreign lobbying sting operation, then, I faced an obvious dilemma: no one would be surprised to discover that Beltway firms would leap at the opportunity to work for a nasty regime if the price was right. The broader goal, of course, was to reveal the particular tricks lobbyists employed, but even so, I wanted to lower the bar as far as possible, ethically speaking, when it came to picking the country that I would allegedly be representing. An exposé of how lobbyists planned to pull the wool over the eyes of an unsuspecting public to further the ambitions of the Canadian government or French dairy producers just wouldn't cut it.

The first step in constructing the cover story was to select a suitably repulsive would-be client, one that would largely be deemed beyond the pale by reasonable observers. That it would be a dictatorial regime was obvious, but it required one that combined just the right mix of crazy and bloodthirsty, topped off with a pinch of the surreal. The whole approach should be slightly outrageous, yet at least remotely plausible, so that I could get, literally or at least figuratively, a foot in the door with the lobbyists.

There was also a question of approach, specifically, reality or comedy. I toyed with the idea of a routine along the lines of Borat, the fictional Kazakh TV reporter and alter ego of British comic Sacha Baron Cohen. In the guise of Borat, Cohen had infuriated the government of Kazakhstan with his portrayal of that country as backward, cruel, and ignorant. "Since the 2003 Tulyakev Reforms, Kazakhstan is as civilized as any other country in the world," Borat said in one pronouncement. "Women can now travel inside of bus. Homosexuals no longer have to wear blue hats. And age of consent has been raised to eight years old. Please, captains of industry, I invite you to come to Kazakhstan, where we have incredible natural resources, hard working labor, and some of the cleanest prostitutes in whole of central Asia."

Borat also attacked Uzbekistan, Kazakhstan's central Asian neighbor, for spreading "disgusting fabrications" about his country (for example, that Kazakhstan treated its women equally and tolerated all religions), and warned that if the propaganda campaign did not cease immediately there would be "no alternative but to commence bombardment of their cities with our catapults." When a Kazakh official threatened to sue Cohen for degrading his country's "ethnic identity," the "Number 2 TOP Television Reporter in Kazakhstan" issued a video reply. Standing beneath a Kazakh flag, he stated, "I'd like to state I have no connection with Mr. Cohen and fully support my government's decision to sue this Jew."

The "moviefilm" *Borat: Cultural Learnings of America for Make Benefit Glorious Nation of Kazakhstan* was a smash hit in the fall of 2006, so a similar shtick had a strong appeal. I could pose as a mildly deranged Eastern European government official who was looking for public relations specialists to defend his nation's honor against charges of abuses by human rights groups. I even envisioned a ridiculous sidekick like the pathetic Azamat, Borat's companion on his journey to America (and co-star in the film's horrific nude wrestling scene).

Yet a stunt like that would clearly have a short run. As amusing as it was to think about, such a scam would clearly lead to a swift bust and prevent my getting a look at how lobbyists pull strings in Washington, which was the whole point.

Only slightly more credible as a potential client was Kim Il Sung, North Korea's Dr. Strangelove. Kim's nuclear aspirations certainly left him in need of a major PR overhaul. In 2002, President Bush had placed North Korea on his "Axis of Evil" along with Iran and Saddam Hussein's Iraq. And with his beehive hairdo, thick glasses, and creepy smile, Kim possessed a cartoon-like villainy. A huge movie buff, Kim had authored *The Art of Cinema*, a turgid, 344-page call for socialist filmmaking. "The task set before the cinema today is one of contributing to people's development into true Communists," he wrote. "This historic task requires, above all, a revolutionary transformation of the practice of directing." How revolutionary? Well, Kim later had South Korean film director Shin Sang Ok and his wife kidnapped and brought to Pyongyang, where, with Dear Leader as executive producer, they were forced to make the classic *Pulgasari: The Legendary Monster.*

But Kim seemed too reviled to be credible, especially as the

United States bans all commerce with North Korea. Even the most crooked lobbyist was unlikely to discuss a deal to work, even indirectly, for Kim. That would risk not merely public opprobrium if exposed, but hard time on the chain gang as well.

Chad, one of the world's poorest nations, was getting closer to the mark. Ruled by Idriss Deby, a warlord who seized power in 1990, the government possessed the requisite embarrassing brutality. The Deby regime tolerates only minor opposition, and its security forces have, with depressing regularity, tortured and killed political opponents. As an added bonus, Chad was in a state of civil war. In early 2006, rebels had nearly overrun the capital, and it briefly looked like doomsday for Deby. But with military support from France and fresh arms purchases, the dictator had fended off the threat and retained power.

While not as extreme as North Korea's Kim, Deby had his share of eccentricities. Despite being a devout Muslim, he was known among diplomats to be a hard drinker and was prone to making outlandish public remarks attacking his enemies, real and imagined. He also sat atop a hugely dysfunctional regime dominated by family members, hacks, and cronies. The president's eldest son, Brahim, had been his chosen successor until 2006, when he was arrested at a Paris disco after a pistol fell out of his pocket during a brawl. A subsequent search of his apartment by the gendarmes yielded Brahim's stash of marijuana and cocaine. The following year Brahim was discovered dead in the garage of his apartment building near Paris. The circumstances were unclear, but police suspected he was murdered.

Another selling point, from my perspective, was that Chad was host to a multi-billion-dollar pipeline project whose partners include ExxonMobil and Chevron. The pipeline, which was supported and underwritten by the World Bank, was supposed to generate revenues and eliminate poverty. The former goal had been achieved—by the end of 2005, less than two years after being inaugurated, the pipeline had earned the state treasury hundreds of millions of dollars—but the latter, predictably, had not. Thanks to massive corruption, little of the money reached ordinary citizens.

Nonetheless, American investment, especially from the politically powerful oil giants, would make Chad more attractive as a client to Washington lobbyists because they would know it could be used to leverage favors from the Bush administration. "The good Lord didn't see fit to put oil and gas only where there are democratic regimes friendly to the United States," Vice President Cheney had once said in explaining why he opposed shunning energy-rich dictators.

But I finally dropped Chad because it was so obscure and remote. Also, while Deby was surely vile, his brand of thuggish rule wasn't notably worse than that of a number of other African despots, including a few that already had Washington representation. The search for the perfect client continued.

I entertained a number of other possibilities, but none seemed quite right. China and Saudi Arabia both had hugely controversial governments, but ties to those countries are well established and each enjoys strong support from American corporate investors and the foreign policy establishment. Furthermore, both China and Saudi Arabia had preexisting contracts with major lobbying firms, so it would be hard for me to explain why I was looking to sign up yet another one. Israel's influence in the United States was controversial, as was its treatment of Palestinians, but it was by no means a pariah in American circles. That an American lobbying firm would offer to work for Israel would come as a shock to no one.

In the end, I settled on the Stalinist regime of Turkmenistan. Before his sudden death in December 2006, President-for-Life

Saparmurat Niyazov built a personality cult that outdid that of any modern leader except possibly Kim of North Korea. "While he lived he was one of the wealthiest and most powerful lunatics on earth," Paul Theroux wrote of Niyazov in a postmortem look at the dictator that ran in *The New Yorker*. "He treated Turkmenistan as his private kingdom, a land in which everything belonged to him."

Niyazov had been named Turkmenistan's Communist boss in 1985 and held on to power after the collapse of the Soviet Union six years later. With the fall of the old regime, the Communists cleverly rebranded themselves the "Democratic Party," and Niyazov was elected president. The balloting was billed as the country's "first free election," though Niyazov ran unopposed and took home 99.5 percent of the vote. A new presidential vote was scheduled for 1997, but that was canceled three years beforehand in a national referendum. The Turkmen authorities reported a turnout of 99.9 percent of the electorate, of whom 99.9 percent agreed that there was no need for a new presidential vote; they wanted Niyazov to remain in power. The inevitable coronation came in 1999, when the People's Council, the country's supreme legislative body, changed the constitution to remove all limits on Niyazov's term of office. In 2002, he was confirmed as President-for-Life.

The People's Council gave Niyazov the title of "Beyik Turkmenbashi," or "the Great Leader of all the Turkmen." He named after himself an entire month of the year (the one we unenlightened non-Turkmen still call January) and another for his beloved late mother, Gurbansolte (April, because plants grow in the spring and we should think of our mothers). The wise leader changed a variety of other names as well. "There is now a Turkmenbashi town (formerly Krasnovodsk), which lies in Turkmenbashi bay, a Turkmenbashi airport, a Turkmenbashi oil refinery, even a Turkmenbashi meteor that landed in Turkmenistan in 1998," Global Witness, a London-based anticorruption group, said in a 2006 report. "In November 1999, a state newspaper seriously suggested that Turkmenistan should be renamed 'Turkmenistan of Saparmurat Turkmenbashi.' "

With vast natural resources, Turkmenistan's prospects seemed bright at independence. However, it didn't take long for the Great Turkmenbashi to run the country's economy into the ground. By 2005, World Bank statistics showed that under his rule, Turkmenistan has progressed the least of the former Soviet republics in terms of economic reforms. Turkmenistan's United Nations Human Development Indicators (HDI), which rate countries on standards of health, education, and quality of living, had been a very respectable 31st in the world when the Turkmenbashi took the reins of power. Within four years it had plunged to 86th—admittedly, this resulted not merely from Niyazov's incompetence but from the overall impact of the state's breakdown with the end of the Communist era—and by 2005 it had further slipped to 97th (out of 177 countries). More than half of the population lived in poverty. Heroin addiction was rampant, as was prostitution.

Not all the news on the economic front was grim, though. There had emerged under Turkmenbashi at least one boom industry: the production of statues of the Leader, which were erected everywhere in the capital of Ashgabat. The most immense was the mammoth Arch of Neutrality, topped by a twelve-foot golden statue of Niyazov that rotates to face the sun. His image adorns billboards and buildings across Turkmenistan, cartons of salt, packets of tea and bottles of vodka and brandy, and immense billboards (which had to be changed every time Turkmenbashi dyed his hair, which was often). "His golden profile also appears in the corner of Turkmen television channels,"

Global Witness reported. "Stories about him feature to such an extent on Turkmen television that people sometimes jokingly say 'change the Niyazov' instead of 'change the channel.' "

Of course, Niyazov personally disapproved of such devotion but was unable to prevent his followers from showering him with their collective affection. Still, it was a sentiment he understood. "If I was a worker and my president gave me all the things they have here in Turkmenistan, I would not only paint his picture, I would have his picture on my shoulder, or on my clothing," he offered modestly during an interview with a Western journalist. He did acknowledge that too many of his portraits, pictures, and monuments were plastered across the country, saying ruefully, "I don't find any pleasure in it, but the people demand it because of their mentality."

When he was crowned as President-for-Life, Niyazov was presented with a white robe and a palm staff, traditional symbols of the Prophet Mohammed. Not long afterward he declared himself a "national prophet," and his emissaries, in an unusual display of sensitivity, queried Islamic embassies in Ashgabat about whether they'd object to his use of that title. To spread his own pearls of personal and spiritual wisdom, Niyazov penned the Ruhnama, which was described on its official website as being "on par with the Bible and the Koran." "Ruhnama is the veil of the Turkmen people's face and soul," Niyazov wrote in the first chapter. "It is the Turkmen's first and basic reference book. It is the total of the Turkmen mind, customs and traditions, intentions, doings and ideals." (For those stimulated to read more, the entire text can be found at a website run by something called the Wentworth Ruhnama Institute, which operates from, of all places, Peoria, Illinois. Here you can purchase themed T-shirts, mugs, and even a Ruhnama tote bag.) September was renamed Ruhnama under the Turkmenbashi, and Saturday was renamed the Day of the Mind, and henceforth was to be devoted to reading his masterwork.

The Ruhnama was translated into several dozen languages—the expense was borne by foreign companies operating in Turkmenistan, as required by the Niyazov regime—ranging from German to Zulu to Braille. The Turkmenbashi's musings never gained much of a readership abroad, but at home, citizens were required to take a sixteen-hour course on the Ruhnama in order to obtain a driver's license and it became the central text in Turkmen education. It was mandatory reading for high school students and formed the basis of foreign language and mathematics lessons. A secondary school math quiz contained questions such as this:

> Gulnara was reading the book *Ruhnama*. She read six pages on the first day. On the second day she read four more pages than on the first day. On the third day she read five pages fewer than on the second day. How many pages of *Ruhnama* did Gulnara read on the third day?

Meanwhile, Niyazov labeled much of school curricula as "obscure" and "disconnected from real life." As a result, the study of Turkmen and world literature was severely reduced or eliminated. Added in their place were courses on the "Politics of Independence of Saparmurat Turkmenbashi the Great" and the Leader's "literary heritage" (consisting, according to one account, "of a collection of his poems and biographies of the President and his parents").

All this might make for mildly if darkly amusing satire, and indeed many have had rich sport in mocking the absurdities of life in Turkmenistan. In *Our Dumb World*, its version of a world atlas, *The Onion* reported that Niyazov had grown even more popular among his Turkmen subjects after his death than he had been in life, and citizens were "bound by law to worship his rotting corpse." According to *Our Dumb World,* the People's Congress had declared Niyazov "President for Afterlife," and the country's most popular TV show remained *Goofing Around,* which was described as "a hilarious comedy in which Niyazov executes those who commit bloopers."

What's less funny, though, is that Niyazov's regime was marked not only by comic-opera madness but (as that last crack suggested) a high level of lethality as well. Any opposition to the Turkmen government was considered to be treason, and thousands of political dissidents have been imprisoned. In 1999, a Turkmen citizen who announced he was forming a political party in Turkmenistan was arrested and jailed after being convicted of embezzling state property. Five years later a man seeking permission to hold a peaceful demonstration was sent to a psychiatric hospital.

Serving in the government offered no protection, as Niyazov was constantly spotting traitors in his midst. He regularly fired ministers and other senior officials, a tactic to ensure that no potential rival emerged to challenge him. "During the year numerous former ministers and government officials were dismissed from their positions, sent into internal exile, placed under house arrest, or sentenced to jail terms," the State Department noted in its 2006 report on global human rights.

The Turkmen national oath—the translation below is from the Ruhnama site—gives a good idea of how dissent was viewed under Niyazov:

> FOR THE SLIGHTEST EVIL AGAINST YOU
> LET MY HAND BE LOST.
> FOR THE SLIGHTEST SLANDER ABOUT YOU
> LET MY TONGUE BE LOST.

AT THE MOMENT OF MY BETRAYAL

TO MY MOTHERLAND,

TO HER SACRED BANNER,

TO SAPARMURAT TÜRKMENBAŞY THE GREAT

LET MY BREATH STOP.

Among independent observers, there was universal condemnation of the Niyazov regime. "Security officials tortured,
routinely beat, and used excessive force against criminal suspects, prisoners, and individuals critical of the government," said
the State Department. A report by a European pro-democracy
group said that in Turkmenistan "the contrast between the law
as it is presented and the reality marked by terror and fright is
mind-boggling." The European Parliament rated Turkmenistan
as "one of the worst totalitarian systems in the world." For eleven
years in a row, Freedom House gave Turkmenistan the lowest
possible scores for both political rights and civil liberties. There
were only seven other countries in that category: Burma, Cuba,
Libya, North Korea, Saudi Arabia, Sudan, and Syria.

More detailed reports of abuses out of Turkmenistan were
bloodcurdling. After an alleged assassination attempt against
Niyazov in 2002, the regime detained and convicted in kangaroo
courts dozens of supposed conspirators. The accused were, said
the State Department, "beaten with water bottles to avoid bruis-
ing, injected with psychotropic drugs, and subjected to electric
shock torture, and . . . their female relatives were sexually as-
saulted and threatened with rape."

In September 2003, a Turkmen Radio Free Europe/Radio
Liberty reporter who had dared to cover the government's
human rights record was arrested and detained for "creating
problems." He was freed after three days but picked up again two
months later. The reporter later said that during his second or-
deal he had been bundled into a car and then beaten and left at

the side of the road. His captors warned him that if he continued to cause trouble he would be buried alive. Taking the hint, the reporter sought and received political asylum in the United States. In 2005, another Radio Free Europe/Radio Liberty reporter, Ogulsapar Muradova, was arrested on trumped-up charges. A month after a kangaroo court convicted her in a secret trial, Muradova, a mother of three, was found dead in her jail cell.

Given this horror show, there were grounds for hope that Niyazov's death—allegedly of cardiac arrest, though other causes, including poisoning, were debated—would mark the onset of a political and economic opening. Yet the early signs were not encouraging. Following the Great Turkmenbashi's demise, Minister of Health Kurbanguly Berdymukhamedov, the former leader's personal dentist, became acting president. Under the constitution, the job was supposed to pass to the speaker of parliament, but he was reportedly arrested soon after Niyazov's death. Some analysts speculated that Berdymukhamedov was the Turkmenbashi's illegitimate son, which would explain his unexpected ascent to the top.

Berdymukhamedov was relatively unknown when he was declared acting president, though he had periodically turned up at the Turkmenbashi's side on state TV. In a 2004 address to students at the Agricultural University in Ashgabat, the Leader offered tips on dental care and said his health minister "will fix you such good teeth." As a beaming Berdymukhamedov looked on, Niyazov dismissed a rumor he described as being fashionable in European capitals—that teeth were strengthened "by eating mincemeat, mashed vegetables or apples, or drinking juice made from them." When it came to dental care, the Leader continued, man should look to his canine companions. "Dogs chew bones not out of hunger but because they contain calcium and fluorine and it is natural," he related. "So guys and girls . . . don't eat whatever comes your way and without paying attention to it. Don't sacrifice yourselves when it comes to your teeth. The harder the substance you chew, the stronger your teeth will become. There are some people who lost their teeth and they lost them because they did not want to eat bones and so on. This is my advice."

As health minister, Berdymukhamedov's own record was not impressive. He had been responsible, according to the BBC, for implementing Niyazov's 2004 health care reforms, which had left the system "near collapse." One of the most controversial of his decrees ordered the closure of all hospitals, except those in Ashgabat and in some major regional towns, and the sacking of 15,000 health care workers and their replacement with untrained army conscripts. Doctors were instructed to forsake the Hippocratic oath and instead pledge their allegiance to—who else?—the Great Turkmenbashi. This undoubtedly helped explain why life expectancy for the average Turkmen had fallen steadily from the Soviet period and as of 2005 was sixty-three, about fifteen years below the average for Europe.

Berdymukhamedov was confirmed as president in an election held in February 2007—he ran against five other candidates, all from the ruling party, and won 89 percent of the vote—in a balloting that he described as being held "on a democratic basis that has been laid by the great [late] leader," but which just about everyone else deemed to be a sham. "His victory was always certain . . . and all official structures worked to ensure the outcome," the International Crisis Group said of Berdymukhamedov's triumph at the polls. In an early interview after becoming president, he said that Niyazov was his role model; as for democracy, he said, "This tender substance cannot be imposed by applying ready imported models. It can be only carefully nurtured by using the wise national experience and traditions of previous generations. You have just witnessed the national presidential elections. What else can serve as a proof of the firm democratic foundations of the society if the Turkmen people elect a new head of state out of six deserving candidates?"

Still, Turkmen held out hope. Even if Berdymukhamedov's election victory was a joke, observers reported enthusiasm among voters. For his part, Berdymukhamedov promised better social services, fewer restrictions on travel and study abroad, and allowing citizens improved access to the Internet. If no one imagined he was likely to be Turkmenistan's version of Mikhail Gorbachev, he seemed—especially when compared to Niyazov—receptive to new ideas.

Yet the bad news far outweighed the good. Two new Internet cafés did open in Ashgabat within days of Berdymukhamedov's inauguration ("one in the solemn Soviet-era Central Telegraph building and the other in a dilapidated telephone exchange station," reported the Associated Press), but there was little business, perhaps because soldiers were posted at the doorways and hourly fees came to the equivalent of about $10, more than the average Turkmen's daily income. A month after Berdymukhamedov took power, the People's Council—the country's highest legislative body, whose twenty-five hundred members all belong to the ruling party—unanimously elected him to be its chairman. Soon, massive Niyazov-style portraits of the new Leader began appearing and state newspapers and TV began singing his praises in the same reverential manner as they had the old Leader. (In the spring of 2008, as I was finishing this book, Berdymukhamedov announced that the Arch of Neutrality would be removed from the center of Ashgabat and relocated to the city's southern outskirts. He also took other encouraging steps, including restoring the names of days and months that the Turkmenbashi had changed to honor of himself and his family.

But Eric McGlinchey, a Turkmen expert at George Mason University, told *The New York Times* that it would be a mistake to read too much into such steps, noting that Berdymukhamedov had also moved to create his own cult of personality, including issuing coins engraved with his image. "I would hesitate to uncork the champagne just yet," McGlinchey told the *Times.* "What he is doing is typical of any new leader trying to remove the legacy of a predecessor and consolidate his hold on power.")

Unlike many of the world's dictatorial regimes, Turkmenistan had no American lobbyists on the payroll. Back in 1993, Niyazov retained retired general Alexander Haig to advise him on winning U.S. business and political support for a natural gas pipeline project that would cross Iran. Haig had served as Richard Nixon's chief of staff and Ronald Reagan's secretary of state, and was best remembered in the latter post for publicly asserting "I am in control here" after Reagan was shot in 1981, though the constitutional chain of command specifies no such thing. Reagan fired Haig after a mere eighteen months on the job. In 1988, the general made his first and only run for public office when he sought the Republican presidential nomination. The most influential person to endorse him was political comedian Mort Sahl. Haig pulled out of the race following the Iowa caucuses, where he finished seventh in a field of six candidates. With 364 votes—0.3 percent—Haig had less than half the tally of the sixth-place finisher, "No preference."

Yet Haig's years in government and the public limelight paved the way for a lucrative career as a Beltway wheeler-dealer. He specialized in opening doors for American corporations seeking to do business overseas, usually in countries headed by dictatorial leaders who were appreciative of the support Haig offered them (or their predecessors) while serving in the Nixon and Reagan administrations. In seeking to sell the pipeline plan to the Clinton administration, Haig reportedly helped arrange a visit by Niyazov to the United States, where he sought to portray his client as a bold reformer. The Turkmen ruler "should be a hero rather than a pariah," Haig told the Associated Press. Haig himself became one of Niyazov's trusted advisers. In 1993, he flew to the Turkmen capital of Ashgabat and appeared on the reviewing stand with Niyazov during independence celebrations. He also joined the Turkmen leader at the head table for a state dinner that was part of the festivities. "For a while there they were joined at the hip," Allen Moore, head of a short-lived outfit called the U.S.-Turkmenistan Business Council, told me of the Haig-Niyazov romance. But the pipeline deal was ultimately blocked by the Clinton administration, which opposed any economic dealings with Iran.

In the mid-1990s, two American lobbying firms signed small, limited deals with the Turkmen government. Chadbourne & Parke sought to enlist American support to help resolve a commercial dispute between Turkmenistan and Ukraine. Meanwhile, the Baltimore law firm of Shapiro & Olander signed a $3,500-per-month deal that for a brief time had it helping Turkmenistan with "foreign policy matters as they affect relations with the United States." As of early 2007, Turkmenistan had not had direct representation in the United States for roughly a decade.

Yes, Turkmenistan was a perfect hellhole, and ideal bait to dangle before my lobbying targets. The fact that Berdymukhamedov had just been "elected" only made the setup better. The new Leader might well see the utility in retaining a lobby shop to seek help in ending Turkmenistan's diplomatic isolation from the United States and its general image as an Eastern European banana republic.

Still, there were kinks to be worked out in the scheme. For example, I couldn't possibly pass as Turkmen, so it would be impossible to approach the lobbying firms as a representative of the government itself. Instead, I decided, I would be a consultant for a Western firm that had a financial stake in Turkmenistan, and a stake as well in improving its public image. Thus was born a mysterious (and wholly fictitious) firm called the Maldon Group. We were, according to the story I ultimately concocted, a group of private investors involved in the export of natural gas from Turkmenistan to Ukrainian and other Eastern European markets. We felt it would strengthen our business position in Turkmenistan if we could convey to American policymakers and journalists just how heady were the winds of change emanating from Ashgabat under the new reformist Berdymukhamedov government, which would, not incidentally, be grateful for our help.

Such cutout arrangements are not unusual. A few years ago, a Washington-area construction and real estate firm called American Worldwide hired the lobbying firm of Patton Boggs to seek foreign aid for the government of Angola, where it was pursuing business deals. Jefferson Waterman used a cutout in its Burma contract and more recently represented the government of Azerbaijan on behalf of Camelot Oil & Gas Development Ltd., an Azeri consulting firm based in London that, a source told me, has close ties to the regime there.

In April 2007 (by which point I was already negotiating with several lobbying firms about representing Turkmenistan), *The Wall Street Journal* reported that Washington insiders were "earning big fees these days by representing controversial clients from the former Soviet Union. In some cases, the details of how these ex-Soviet clients made their fortunes are murky." The *Journal* cited the 2004 case of Foruper Ltd., "a United Kingdom shell company . . . which had no assets or employees," that paid the lobbying firm Barbour Griffith & Rogers $820,000 in fees for "promotion of greater cooperation and financial ties between Eastern Europe and the West."

If shilling for Turkmenistan did not in itself trouble the lobbying firms, my description of the Maldon Group was designed to raise a number of bright red flags. Turkmenistan has vast reserves of natural gas, from which it earns about $2 billion per year in export revenues. Most exported Turkmen gas is sold to Ukraine, and growing volumes are resold from there to European countries such as Poland and Germany. Ukraine has historically paid for much of its Turkmen gas supplies not in cash, but through the barter of chemicals, food, raw materials, and machinery. Turkmen gas can reach Ukraine only via pipelines controlled by Russia's Gazprom, the world's largest gas company.

The whole business has been marked by flagrant corruption—as could be ascertained very quickly by anyone who cared to perform a Google search. The 2006 study by Global Witness reported that Niyazov kept billions of dollars in gas revenues under his effective control in overseas accounts. Among the troubling problems pointed to in the report was that while Gazprom controlled the export pipelines, it didn't ship the gas itself. Instead, that highly profitable business was taken over by a number of murky intermediary companies—upon which I modeled the Maldon Group—who almost surely paid off Gazprom insiders for the privilege. "These companies have often come out of nowhere, parlaying tiny amounts of start-up capital into billion-dollar deals," Global Witness said. "Their ultimate beneficial ownership has been hidden behind complex networks of trusts, holding companies and nominee directors and there is almost no public information about where their profits go."

The first intermediary firm to appear on the scene, back in the mid-1990s, was Respublika, which swapped Ukrainian goods for Turkmen gas in a series of bizarre barter deals. One curious enterprise involved an energy-for-galoshes exchange; Turkmenistan received twelve million pairs, three pairs per citizen of the desert country. Respublika's head, Ihor Bakai, later became head of the Ukrainian state energy company. At that post, he came under suspicion of corruption, fled the country, and is still wanted by Ukrainian authorities.

Then there was an intermediary firm called Itera (we'll be hearing more about it later), whose top managers included a former deputy prime minister of Turkmenistan. For a period, Gazprom was one of Itera's customers, choosing to pay the company prices far above the rate at which it could have made purchases directly from Turkmenistan. Next up was Eural Trans Gas (ETG), which was founded in Hungary in late 2002 with a mere $12,000 in the bank. The day after it was founded, ETG received a billion-dollar contract to transport Turkmen gas to Ukraine.

RosUkrEnergo, the latest intermediary firm to appear on the scene, is registered in Switzerland and co-owned by Gazprom and an Austrian firm called Raiffeisen Investment. The latter manages its share on behalf of a consortium of Ukrainian businessmen who have refused to disclose their identities. Three murky British businessmen have held posts at RosUkrEnergo, including two who were also involved with its predecessor firm, ETG. *The Washington Post* reported that an American company that explored doing business with RosUkrEnergo performed a due diligence investigation and "uncovered links to more than 140 offshore companies and trusts, from remote island nations such as Nauru and the Seychelles to Cyprus and Panama." The *Post* said that RosUkrEnergo existed only because of its connections, not any expertise it offered. The paper spoke with one international consultant who estimated that RosUkrEnergo had "earned hundreds of millions of dollars for transactions that could easily have been handled by the [Ukrainian] state oil and gas company."

Though I wouldn't say so directly in pitching the lobbyists, my description of the Maldon Group would match the modus operandi of these already existing intermediary firms and all but identify my fake company as one of the fast-and-loose business ventures that have plundered Eastern Europe following the fall of Communism. Since British businessmen had been identified as having key roles at several of the intermediary firms, the Maldon Group's London address would be another tip-off of potential trouble to the lobbying firms I approached. Surely they would want to perform some rigorous due diligence checks before pondering a business relationship with my company.

As a test of the inherent sleaziness of my proposition, I contacted Tom Mayne, the Turkmen expert at Global Witness, and pretended that in the course of conducting research about the Turkmenistan natural gas trade, I had stumbled across a company called the Maldon Group. I gave him the relevant details and asked him if there were grounds to merit further investigation. "Anything having to do with the export of natural gas from Turkmenistan to Ukraine has a big question mark surrounding it," he told me. "If the firm is being quite secretive, that would raise more red flags, especially if there's very little known about it."

In its 2006 report, Global Witness had said that despite "public concerns about official corruption and organized crime in the countries of the former Soviet Union," there had never been proper oversight of the intermediary companies that had dominated the Turkmen gas trade. It was "nigh on impossible to discover who sits at the centre of these corporate webs and thus to whom the profits from the transportation and sale of natural gas are going," the report said. An investigation was urgently needed.

Such an investigation, of course, would be problematic for both the Turkmen government and a company like the Maldon Group. It was time to call in the lobbyists.

THREE

K Street:
The Fourth Branch of Government

BY NOW, MOST OF AMERICA IS FAMILIAR WITH THE TALE OF Jack Abramoff, the super-lobbyist and convicted fraudster who has come to personify Washington sleaze. During the course of his prodigious career, Abramoff bought influence with lawmakers and congressional staffers through lavish campaign contributions, skybox seats at sporting events, and free meals at Signatures, his tony restaurant on Pennsylvania Avenue a few blocks from the White House, which offered clients "liberal portions," such as a plate-size $74 steak, "in a conservative setting." He illegally funneled huge sums to his political allies and causes through a maze of front operations and, most notoriously, bilked tens of millions of dollars out of his Native American tribal clients (whom he described in private e-mails to colleagues as "monkeys," "troglodytes," and "idiots").

"We are missing the boat," Abramoff wrote in a 2002 e-mail to Michael Scanlon, his partner in working the tribes and a former aide to then House majority leader Tom DeLay. "There are a ton of potential opportunities out there," he wrote in another e-mail. "There are 27 tribes which make more than $100 [million] a year. . . . We need to get moving on them. . . . I think the key thing to remember with all these clients is that they are annoying, but that the annoying losers are the only ones which have this kind of money and part with it so quickly."

Abramoff's tactics as a lobbyist mirrored the strategy of Basil Zaharoff, the early-twentieth-century arms dealer. Zaharoff once sold a submarine to Greece and then terrified the Turks so much with tales of its enemy's sinister new vessel that they bought two of their own. Abramoff, too, was an expert at playing both sides. In one case, he and his friend Ralph Reed, the founder of the Christian Coalition, quietly worked in support of Texas attorney general John Cornyn's efforts to shut down a casino called Speaking Rock, which was operated by the Tigua tribe. Then he pitched his services to the Tiguas, who hired him and paid him $4.2 million over the next several years. Abramoff won a provision—slipped into a bill by a friendly congressman—that temporarily reversed the closure of the casino, but in the end Texas succeeded in shutting it down and the Tiguas were out their money.

The key to Abramoff's success was his entrée with powerful people. The Center for Public Integrity reported that he had raised at least $100,000 for Bush-Cheney '04 and lobbied the executive branch for nineteen clients. Abramoff was intimate with onetime majority leader Tom DeLay on the basis of similar financial incentives, as well as his hiring of Scanlon and other DeLay staffers, and by sending DeLay to play golf in Scotland, visit South Korea, and meet Russian oil tycoons in Moscow.

Abramoff's lobbying team and clients also contributed more than $140,000 to the campaign coffers of Senator Conrad Burns of Montana, who chaired a committee with oversight over the Bureau of Indian Affairs. Team Abramoff paid for gifts and trips for several of Burns's staffers, two of whom subsequently went to work for Abramoff. The relationship was mutually beneficial. "Every appropriation we wanted [from Burns's committee] we got," Abramoff later said. "Our staffs were as close as they could be. They practically used Signatures as their cafeteria."

Burns lost his seat in the 2006 elections, in large measure owing to his relationship with Abramoff. But in January 2008 the Justice Department closed an investigation of Burns's dealings with the lobbyist and decided not to bring charges. By then, Burns was himself working as a lobbyist, at a firm called Gage, which had been founded by a group of his former staffers.

Abramoff, of course, was ultimately exposed—with help from lobbying competitors who ratted him out to the press— and is now a convicted felon. But what's particularly remarkable about the whole Abramoff affair is that over the course of his lobbying career, Jack didn't generally need to break the law. That's because the real scandal in Washington, as the writer Michael Kinsley once remarked, is not what's illegal, but what's legal. Well-connected, cash-dispensing lobbyists winning favors for their clients, be they private business interests or foreign dictators, is by now a routine, predictable, and accepted outcome of the American political process.

Which was precisely what I hoped to illustrate with the Turkmeniscam sting.

THE ORIGIN OF THE TERM "LOBBYIST" IS NOT ENTIRELY CLEAR, THOUGH its earliest use seems to be a derogatory reference to hangers-on who gathered in the lobbies of legislative assemblies in hopes of having a word with lawmakers. The website of the American League of Lobbyists cites an early-nineteenth-century account of "lobby-agents" waiting for legislators in the lobby of the New York state capitol, and another that described the lobby of the Willard Hotel as a favored spot for official favor seekers. "Either way, by 1835 the term had been shortened to 'lobbyist' and was in wide usage in the U.S. Capitol, though frequently pejoratively," says the website.

Wherever the term comes from, the practice itself dates to the very earliest days of the Republic. Already in 1792, veterans of the War of Independence had retained an agent, William Hull, to seek additional compensation for their war services. Three years later, a Philadelphia newspaper reported on the growing numbers of people loitering outside Congress Hall to "give a hint to a Member, teaze or advise as may best suit." Washington at the time was a cow town that "bore no resemblance to the cosmopolitan centers of Philadelphia and New York, let alone the great European capitals," Senator Robert Byrd said in a 1987 address about the history of Congress.

> The city was dusty and malaria-ridden in the summer, damp and cold in the winter. Social and cultural amenities were few. Many senators left their families at home and took rooms in the boardinghouses that surrounded the Capitol Building. It was an atmosphere in which the so-called "social lobby" could thrive, and thrive it did. Clubs, brothels, and "gambling dens" became natural habitats of the lobbyists, since these institutions were occasionally visited by members of Congress, who, far from home, came seeking good food, drink, and agreeable company.

As early as the closing years of the eighteenth century, Byrd reports, the activities of lobbyists helped arouse "widespread suspicions that large, well-financed interests were receiving special attention from the government."

By 1852, future president James Buchanan was already complaining in a letter to another future president, Franklin Pierce, about the "host of contractors, speculators, stock jobbers and lobby members which haunt the halls of Congress." One scandal from this period involved a lobbyist for the famous gun maker Samuel Colt, who in seeking to win a patent extension for his paymaster wooed wavering senators with gifts of pistols as well as lavish entertainment. A subsequent congressional investigation characterized the lobbyist's guiding principle as "To reach the heart or get the vote / The surest way is down the throat."

The influence of lobbyists continued to grow in the aftermath of the Civil War. A newspaper description from 1869 spoke metaphorically of a demon that wound "in and out through the long, devious basement passage [of the Capitol building], crawling through the corridors, trailing its slimy length from gallery to committee room, at last it lies stretched at full length on the floor of Congress—this dazzling reptile, this huge, scaly serpent of the lobby."

Sam Ward, known as the "King of the Lobby," worked for a host of corporations and foreign governments. He was also employed by the Treasury Department to lobby lawmakers on financial policies it favored. Like Colt's lobbyists, Ward provided members of Congress with bountiful offerings of food and drink. He "proceeded upon the comfortable axiom that the shortest distance between a pending bill and a Congressman's 'aye' lies through his stomach," Ward's biographer wrote.

In 1875, Ward testified during a congressional investigation of subsidies won by a steamship company. "This business of lobbying, so called, is as precarious as fishing in the Hebrides," Ward, who was not charged with any wrongdoing in the affair, told lawmakers. "You get all ready, your boats go out—suddenly there comes a storm, and away you are driven. . . . Everybody who knows anything about Washington knows that ten times, aye, fifty times, more measures are lost than are carried; but once in a while a pleasant little windfall of this kind recompenses us, who are always toiling here, for the disappointments."

By the 1920s, Byrd said in his speech, "Washington lobbying had begun to develop many of the features we associate with it today. Lobbying broadened its scope beyond financial and commercial interests, and the free-lance lobbyist was supplanted by collective action in the form of membership associations, which had been growing and developing since the beginning of the century." Influence peddling scandals erupted regularly, but members of Congress, who as they do today benefited so much from lobbyists' largesse, failed to act until World War II came to a close, at which point the public demanded action.

Following hearings at which the American Political Science Association proposed some form of disclosure laws, saying that Congress was "handicapped in the performance of its proper function . . . by the importunities of special-interest groups which tend to divert legislative emphasis from broad questions of public interest," lawmakers in 1946 approved a major reform bill. The legislation required lobbyists to reveal in quarterly reports their clients, fees, and legislative aims, as well as their political contributions of $500 or more and the names of newspapers and magazines in which they "caused to be published" articles or editorials.

DESPITE PASSAGE OF THE REFORM BILL, THE LOBBYING TRADE CONTINued to expand steadily. It was only during the past quarter century, though, that the industry exploded. Today, downtown Washington is overrun with lobby shops, consulting firms, and public relations companies, which collectively form a fourth branch of government. There are now some 30,000 registered lobbyists at work in Washington—more than fifty for every member of Congress—and a 2008 *Washington Post* story put the true number, including support staff, at a staggering 261,000. Between 1975 and 2006, total revenues for Beltway lobbying firms climbed from less than $100 million per year to roughly $2.5 billion. (This doesn't include vast payments made to PR firms or for "grassroots" lobbying, an industry described below.)

The rapid growth of the influence peddling industry occurred because business leaders—spurred into action by the populist upsurges of the 1960s and 1970s, especially anticorporate campaigns led by Ralph Nader and the more general upheavals surrounding the Vietnam War and the Watergate scandal—became far more aggressive in seeking to influence government policy. In the early 1970s, most big companies didn't even maintain Washington offices. Today, thousands of corporations and national trade and business membership groups operate in the capital. Most of these companies and organizations run in-house lobby shops, while depending on hired guns from outside firms to provide supplemental firepower. Another factor behind the industry's expansion, as the *Post* story cited above noted, has been "an extension of the growth and reach of government. The ballooning federal budget has its tentacles in every aspect of American life and commerce. No serious industry or interest can function without monitoring, and at least trying to manipulate, Washington's decision makers."

The world of lobbying has been transformed during recent decades at the tactical level as well. Until as recently as two decades ago, lobbyists dispensed vast sums of money to directly subsidize the day-to-day life of elected officials. The former head of Grumman's Washington offices, Gordon Ochenrider, filed a disclosure form in 1986 that revealed $12,093 worth of meals, liquor, flowers, Kennedy Center entertainment, fees at the Washington Golf and Country Club, and tickets to sporting events. "Christmas used to be a wild time," Jake Lewis, a longtime staffer to two legendary Texas populists, Congressmen Wright Patman and Henry González, once told me. "Lobbyists would drop by the offices with buckets of booze, cigarettes, and other goodies. They'd pass out plenty of stuff unless you turned them down, and there were few who did."

The straightforward cash prize was long an accepted practice as well. "Back in the old days, it was a common occurrence that [lobbyists] walked around with envelopes of cash in their pockets," J. D. Williams, a lobbyist and former aide to deceased Oklahoma senator Robert S. Kerr, once explained to *Legal Times*. "One time I had mistakenly given a fairly junior member of a committee the envelope for the chairman of the committee. I sensed this when I received a call from the [junior] committee member saying how nice it was, what I'd done, and that I 'knew we were friends but I didn't know we were that good.' "

The death of a longtime congressman, a powerful member of the important Ways and Means committee whom Williams described only as "a crusty old guy from the South," offered a glimpse of just how much money was being tossed at lawmakers by lobbyists: "Everyone in Longworth [House Office Building] had a little brown safe in the wall, and when he died, they opened this guy's safe," he recounted. "And they took shoebox after shoebox of $100 bills out of that safe." (Williams was long one of the Beltway's most influential lobbyists. In 1989, *The Wall Street Journal* reported that the manager of a federal wildlife refuge had fined Williams for allegedly downing too many ducks. The lobbyist made some phone calls and the manager was reassigned.)

Lobbyists have periodically employed other powerful lures in seeking to influence lawmakers. In Ronald Kessler's book *In-*

side Congress, longtime Senate staffer Roy Elson recalled that for many years there was a "cathouse" not far from the congressional office buildings. Some members of Congress were known to frequent it, courtesy of lobbyists who picked up the tab.

An agricultural lobbyist named Paula Parkinson preferred a more direct approach to the matter of sex and political influence. Back in 1981, she traveled to Florida for a vacation with three members of the House, Thomas Evans, Tom Railsback, and future vice president Dan Quayle. The quartet shared a cottage and golfed. Upon returning to Washington, the three congressmen became intensely interested in the topic of federal crop insurance. They soon cast votes against a piece of legislation that Parkinson was being paid to block.

The golfing vacation was duly exposed, and an investigation ensued about whether the congressmen had traded their votes for sex. All denied it, but Evans was forced to fess up to having an affair with Parkinson. He said he regretted his "association" with the lobbyist and, like many before and after him in similar situations, asked for God's and his family's forgiveness. It's not clear how those requests were received, but his constituents were not in a forgiving mood, and voted him out of office at the first opportunity. (It was rumored that Parkinson had videotaped sexual encounters with other members of Congress. This gave rise in Washington to the term "Parkinson's disease," owing, it was said, to the fact that congressmen would begin shaking at the mere mention of her name. Meanwhile, Parkinson's husband publicly apologized for creating a "sexual Frankenstein.")

Sponsoring junkets, especially to exotic overseas locations, was another routine manner by which lobbyists curried favor with lawmakers. In 1990, ABC's *Prime Time Live* caught a group of nine House members, along with family members and aides, at a resort in Barbados. Taxpayers picked up the cost of transportation to the island and hotel bills, while corporate lobbyists who had accompanied the junketeers helped cover daily expenses. In one scene filmed by *Prime Time,* a lobbyist and former congressman puffed on a cigar as he pulled a wad of bills out of his pocket to pay for Jet Ski rides for two members of the delegation.

Hill staffers, especially senior ones on key committees such as Appropriations and Defense, also traveled widely. "You knew you were a hitter when you got invited on big overseas trips to places like China," one former Hill denizen told me. "You'd work for a half hour and then go on tours, and stop off at the pearl market." This person knew staffers who picked issues to get involved with on the basis of the corresponding junkets. "If they wanted to see the shuttle launch from Cape Canaveral, they'd become interested [in NASA]," she said. Some staffers she knew also developed a strong interest in farming issues after hearing about one regularly scheduled junket. "The University of Florida Agriculture Department would fly them down to see an orange grove or a tomato farm and then it would be off to Joe's Crab Shack for a booze fest," she recounted.

This truly was the golden age of lobbying, as *Campaigns & Elections* magazine once described it. "There was a time when lobbying was strictly a back room affair," the magazine wrote. "Affable men in suits would hang around swarming, sweaty, legislative chambers, button-holing lawmakers, as they swaggered through lustrous brown doors, whispering in ears, slapping backs, winking knowingly. These were the same men who were always good for a free lunch, a round of cocktails, and at election time, a check from their faint-hearted clients."

This backroom world is far from extinct, but lobbyists developed new tactics as legal restrictions and tighter disclosure rules dampened the effectiveness of past techniques. Cash bribes passed under the table were replaced by campaign checks passed across the table. In a similar transition, junkets to cushy resorts gave way to "fact-finding missions," on which lawmakers gave a speech or appeared on a panel in exchange for room and board at the same cushy resorts.

Growing public cynicism about the influence of big business led lobbyists to disguise their clients' direct involvement in campaigns. The most direct consequence has been the explosion of fake "grassroots" mobilizations. Back in 1993, Burson Marsteller was hired by the oil industry to help build opposition to an energy tax proposed by President Bill Clinton. A company executive, Jim McAvoy, was charged with coordinating rallies in small towns across the country. Just a decade earlier, the energy industry could have killed the tax with a handful of Beltway lobbyists, McAvoy lamented to the press at the time. "Now you have to hire 45 people and send them to 23 states because all the noise is supposed to have more credibility."

By 1995, grassroots lobbying (dubbed "AstroTurf" by critics) had become an $800 million industry, according to *Campaigns & Elections* magazine. That same year, Congress gave the industry a big boost by exempting grassroots lobbyists from new disclosure requirements, after conservative groups, led by the Christian Coalition, argued that they would amount to an assault on free speech.

Defense contractor Northrop Grumman twice employed the grassroots firm of Bonner & Associates to protect funding for the B-2 bomber, which at $2 billion per plane is the most costly item of military equipment ever designed. While a technological marvel, the B-2 was plagued by cost overruns and embarrassing glitches. The Government Accountability Office once reported that the stealth plane's radar system could not distinguish between a rain cloud and a mountainside.

This was not, hard though it may be to believe, the routine's low point. Even more bloodcurdling was a song to the tune of Sister Sledge's "We Are Family." The lyrics were flashed on a screen so the audience could sing along:

We are Franchisees,
We make Double Whoppers with Cheese,
We are Franchisees,
Get off your broiled patties and sing!

Public Policy Associates knows whereof it sings. During the past decade, the company's own PAC and officials doled out well over a million dollars in political contributions.

A FULL TAXONOMY OF THE LOBBYISTS OF WASHINGTON WOULD NECES-sitate a book-length field guide, but a few of the more salient species can be considered here. Perhaps the most effective lobbyists are those actually related, by blood or marriage, to a powerful member of Congress. Public Citizen's Congress Watch found in 2006 that at least three dozen members of Congress have relatives who are professional lobbyists. For years many Alaskan firms, and even huge corporations such as Lockheed Martin, retained the services of William Bittner, brother-in-law of Senator Stevens. In one case, Stevens inserted a single line into a bill that awarded $9.6 million to a program whose chief beneficiary was a Hyundai subsidiary represented by Bittner.

The lobbyist-relatives (and those who hire them) invariably insist that they get hired purely because of their vast talents and insights, not because of their blood ties to powerful political figures. Rarely does that argument withstand even cursory scrutiny. Take, for example, Randolph "Randy" DeLay, the brother of former House powerhouse Tom DeLay. Until the early 1990s, Randy's financial prospects were grim indeed. Four business ventures in which he was involved—a restaurant, two oil projects, and investments in beach property—had gone under. Shareholders in one of the oil ventures sued DeLay in a dispute that was later settled out of court. In another case, DeLay's uncle and four other business partners sold a company called Oilfield Distribution out from under Randy, and the new owner fired him from his $120,000-per-year post as the firm's CEO. As a result of these setbacks, DeLay filed for bankruptcy in 1992.

Salvation came in early 1995, when Tom was elected to the post of House whip. A number of big firms and trade associations promptly began to hire Randy as a lobbyist, though he had no previous experience. His clients included Houston Lighting and Power; Cemex, the Mexican cement monopoly; Union Pacific Railroad; and the city of Houston, which is home to both DeLays. Between 1995 and mid-1997, Randy DeLay earned $750,000 in fees and expenses. The man who just five years earlier had been forced to seek refuge in bankruptcy now had a plush office in a Houston high-rise and regularly flew to Washington to meet with his clients.

But Randy's fortunes, at least as a lobbyist, apparently tanked again after brother Tom became embroiled in various political scandals and lost his seat in Congress. As of late 2007, the only client for whom he was formally registered was a Houston firm called Motor Coach Industries, which had paid him $60,000 for the first half of the year.

Fraternal bonds also enhanced the lobbying career of Kit Murtha, the brother of Congressman John Murtha, the Pennsylvania Democrat and perennial powerhouse on the House Appropriations Defense Subcommittee. When Congress passed the Pentagon's mammoth budget in 2005, Congressman Murtha boasted about all the money he secured to create jobs in his district. He didn't mention that the bill he helped write also benefited at least ten companies represented by KSA, where brother Kit was retained as a lobbyist. KSA's top officials also include Carmen Scialabba, who had previously worked as a congressional aide to Murtha for twenty-seven years.

The ten KSA clients received a total of $20.8 million from the bill. One, a small Arkansas maker of military vehicles, received $1.7 million—triple its total sales for 2004. Mobilvox Inc. received $1.7 million to develop a "knowledge management" system for the Navy called Cognitive Warrior. That was a huge financial boost for a company with 2004 sales of $2.5 million. Rick Ianieri of Coherent Systems, another KSA client, hired the firm on the advice of John Hugya, Congressman Murtha's chief of staff. "I told him we were a new company and needed representation," Ianieri told me at the time. "He threw out a few names but said [KSA] was the [firm] to talk to."

Kit Murtha had at least worked as a lobbyist in the past, for Westinghouse, before being recruited by KSA. Karen Weldon, the daughter of former congressman Curt Weldon of Pennsylvania, had no professional credentials when she opened a lobby shop called Solutions North America in 2002. Karen—whose partner at Solutions was Charles Sexton, Jr., her father's former campaign finance chairman—had an undergraduate degree in education and a graduate degree in information systems. She had spent six years working for Boeing, which has a helicopter plant located near Congressman Weldon's district and was a frequent beneficiary of his work in Washington as well as one of his top campaign donors.

Within six months of hanging out its shingle, Solutions had signed up a million dollars' worth of contracts with three clients: a wealthy Serbian family, the Karićs, that had been linked to accused war criminal Slobodan Milošević and were hoping to win

visas to enter the United States; a Russian aerospace manufac-
turer; and a Russian natural gas company, Itera International
Energy Corp.

Karen got the first contract after Congressman Weldon
championed (unsuccessfully in the end) the efforts of Dragomir
and Bogoljub Karić to win U.S. visas from the State Department.
Weldon had been warned by American officials that the broth-
ers were too close to Milošević, but he praised them as model
business leaders and humanitarians who had been victims of
faulty intelligence reports. At one point, Karen Weldon's firm
paid for her father's chief of staff to take a "fact-finding" trip to
Serbia, where he met with American embassy officials about the
Karićs' visa problems. (House ethics rules bar members of Congress or their aides from taking official trips paid for by lobbyists. The chief of staff reimbursed Solutions with his own money
after questions were raised about the trip.)

Karen's second client, Saratov Aviation Plant, hired her firm
for $20,000 a month after her dad pitched the company's saucer-
shaped drone to the U.S. Navy, which signed a letter of intent to
invest in the technology. Weldon, who chaired a subcommittee
that oversaw $60 billion in military acquisitions, then sought
funding for the project.

The Maldon Group, the firm I created for the Turkmeniscam
operation, was loosely modeled on Solutions' third client, the
shady Russian natural gas firm called Itera. Investment fund
managers with interests in Eastern Europe and numerous press
accounts had suggested that Gazprom, the state-controlled Russian conglomerate, had transferred billions of dollars' worth of
natural gas resources to Itera and received little or nothing in return. Gazprom insiders involved in those transfers were alleged
to have received massive kickbacks.

The controversy has been a cloud over Itera's efforts to gain
access to Western investment capital and markets. In March

2002, the U.S. Trade and Development Agency withdrew an $868,000 grant to the company after questions were raised about Itera's background. It was a major setback to the firm, which had been seeking to expand its natural gas holdings in the United States.

So Itera was badly in need of an image overhaul when Congressman Weldon rode to the rescue that spring, leading a congressional delegation to Moscow in connection with a visit by President Bush. He toured Itera's offices and, according to a company news release, praised it as a "strong and well-established company" and recommended it as "a great source" for U.S. energy firms seeking partners for joint ventures. When he returned home, Weldon attacked the Trade and Development Agency's decision at a news conference and made calls to the State Department on the company's behalf, though to no avail.

In early September 2002, Itera paid for Weldon's lodging in New York, where a Russian radio program interviewed him about energy issues. Meanwhile, Karen had been negotiating a lobbying deal with Itera. Shortly after her father returned from New York, Itera sent Karen an e-mail informing her the company would complete the terms of a half-million-dollar contract at an upcoming dinner in Washington that her father was co-hosting to honor Itera's chairman.

Events moved quickly over the next few months. In rapid succession:

- The dinner took place at the Library of Congress.
- Congressman Weldon introduced a resolution in the House that encouraged U.S.-Russian cooperation on developing energy resources.
- In a floor speech, Weldon gave House colleagues a glowing report on Itera.

- Itera signed the $500,000-a-year contract with Solutions, which agreed to work on creating "good public relations so in the future Itera may sell goods and services to U.S. entities."
- Weldon led a congressional delegation to Eastern Europe. Itera paid for Karen Weldon to join him. Father and daughter met with the president of Georgia, and the congressman helped Itera resolve a costly commercial dispute with the Georgian government. During a stop in Moscow, Weldon called for increased U.S. imports from Itera and other Russian energy corporations.

By early 2003, Itera had enough confidence in its prospects here to open an expanded U.S. headquarters in Jacksonville, Florida. The company flew the congressman down for the gala marking the event. "I can think of no other company that represents what Russia is today and offers for the future," the congressman told the crowd.

Three years later, the FBI raided Solutions North America's offices due to suspicions (first raised in a *Los Angeles Times* story I co-authored) about her firm's links to her father. Voters in Weldon's suburban Philadelphia district soon voted him out of office, but the congressman wasn't out of work for long. Defense Solutions, a military contractor headquartered in his old district and with offices in Eastern Europe, soon put him on the payroll. Weldon also opened up his own business consulting firm, using the contacts he established with foreign leaders while in Congress as an asset to entice clients.

RETIRED ADMINISTRATION OFFICIALS, MEMBERS OF CONGRESS, AND Hill staffers make particularly effective lobbyists since they so often have formed close ties with and enjoy easy access to the colleagues they left behind. And lobbying is an alluring field for lawmakers and staffers since it offers the prospect of a swift boost in income. Oregon senator Bob Packwood stepped down as chairman of the Senate Finance Committee in 1996 over allegations of sexual harassment made by female staffers, colleagues, and reporters. While still a senator, Packwood had confided to his fatal diaries that he regarded the Senate, where he dwelled for twenty-seven years, as but a stepping-stone to a more lucrative career as an influence peddler. Perhaps someday, he mused, "I can become a lobbyist at five or six or four hundred thousand" dollars a year. Less than a year after he resigned in disgrace, Packwood formed a firm called Sunrise Research and was making lavish fees representing timber firms and other corporate clients seeking lower business taxes.

As the Packwood story suggests, public disgrace in Congress is no obstacle to a profitable career as a lobbyist. To cite an older but particularly striking example, Representative Robert Leggett of California became a successful lobbyist even though he was forced to give up his House seat after acknowledging that he'd sired two illegitimate children by a congressional secretary, had another affair with an aide to Speaker Carl Albert, and forged his wife's name to a document transferring title of their home. "In the lobbying world, developing a reputation as something of a rascal isn't necessarily negative—[as long as] you can deliver the bridge, or the vice president, to your client," *Washingtonian* magazine writes. "What matters on this turf is winning."

In April 2005, the Center for Public Integrity revealed that more than twenty-two hundred former federal government employees had registered as lobbyists between 1998 and 2004, of whom hundreds were retired members of Congress and staffers. Consider here the case of just one, Gregory Nickerson, and a huge $140 billion corporate tax break Congress passed in 2004 with the Orwellian name of the American Jobs Creation Act. Described by Senator John McCain as "the worst example of the influence of special interests that I have ever seen," the bill's six-hundred-plus pages were chock-full of pork for pharmaceutical companies, the tobacco industry, cruise ship operators, and defense firms, among others.

Nickerson at the time was tax counsel to Congressman Bill Thomas, the California Republican who then headed the House Ways and Means Committee and was a key architect of the bill. And guess who became a lobbyist almost as soon as the ink was dry on the act and immediately began signing up firms who benefited from his handiwork?

Correct. Nickerson is now a principal with Angus & Nickerson, a consulting firm that "identifies tax issues, crafts legislative solutions, works with Congress to get legislation enacted, and resolves issues through the regulatory process by working with Treasury and the Internal Revenue Service." Nickerson left his job at Ways and Means in February 2005, which is the same month that Angus & Nickerson signed up its first client.

The American Jobs Creation Act's key measure was a one-time provision that reduced the corporate tax rate on overseas earnings from 35 percent to 5.25 percent. When it was being debated, the Ways and Means Committee released a list of firms that supported the act. The list included General Electric, Hewlett-Packard, Procter & Gamble, and Johnson & Johnson, all of which are estimated to have netted multi-billion-dollar savings as a result of the act's passage.

General Electric signed up with Angus & Nickerson just weeks after it opened for business. GE, the firm's second client, paid the lobby shop $120,000 for 2005, a real steal given its tax savings under the act. The other three companies mentioned above also retained Angus & Nickerson, though they waited a few more months—perhaps for appearance's sake—before doing so.

Many other firms show up on both the Ways and Means Committee list of American Jobs Creation Act advocates and Angus & Nickerson's client list. Among them are Coca-Cola (the firm's third client, which retained the lobby shop for "general representation on tax issues before Congress and the administration, including issues under the American Jobs Creation Act of 2004"), Alpharam (fourth), Time Warner (ninth), Citigroup (tenth), Caterpillar, Northrop Grumman, Pepsico, and Wal-Mart. In other words, Nickerson helped write the tax code and then richly profited from his government employment by helping private companies benefit from the very loopholes he inserted.

Supporters of the American Jobs Creation Act had argued that with all their tax savings, the companies that benefited would rush out and hire lots of new workers. But it didn't turn out that way. "One thing is clear," *BusinessWeek* reported in August 2005. "The money piling in from abroad as the result of the Jobs Creation Act has done little to actually spur hiring. In fact, six of the 10 companies repatriating the biggest totals are axing workers in the U.S. They include HP [Hewlett-Packard], which announced July 19 that it would cut its head count by 14,500 in the U.S."

White House and federal branch employees are just as quick to cash in on their public sector experience as members of Congress and Hill staffers. In fact, Nickerson's new lobbying partner is Barbara Angus. She left her job at the Treasury Department— she served as international tax counsel for the Office of Tax Policy—the same month as Nickerson left his.

The "revolving door" is surely not unique to the administration of George W. Bush, but it's been spinning like a pinwheel since he took office. Top officials involved in energy policy are among those who have moved through it with particular alacrity and profitability, which is no surprise given the administration's pro-industry stance. One notable revolver is Francis Blake, who served a mere ten months as a deputy secretary for the U.S. Department of Energy before retiring from that post in March 2002. While in government, he helped to craft the White House's National Energy Plan and led an interagency review of a Clean Air Act program. The review called for a steep reduction in lawsuits against the owners of old, highly polluting coal-fired power plants and instead favored incentives for companies that voluntarily reduced toxic emissions.

Two years after leaving his government job, Blake was named to the board of Southern Co., which had been one of the biggest beneficiaries, and advocates, of the changes that Blake had implemented. Southern Co. was a major contributor to a lobbying campaign that successfully sought an end to still-active Clinton-era lawsuits against the coal companies. A number of Southern's plants had been targeted for legal action before Blake stepped in.

Carl Michael Smith, a former president of the Oklahoma Independent Petroleum Association, was assistant secretary for fossil energy between 2002 and 2004. While in government, he pushed to promote oil drilling wherever a drop might be found, saying that improved technology would allow for "exploration and drilling [that] would leave virtually no lasting trace on the surface." Among the areas he wanted explored was Alaska's Arctic National Wildlife Refuge. "It looks like the Sahara covered by snow," Smith said of complaints the drilling would damage the Alaskan wilderness. "It's simply a non-issue with me."

Shortly before retiring from the Energy Department, Smith attended a four-thousand-dollar-a-head event at an Arizona resort where energy industry executives golfed and dined with key congressional Republicans and administration officials. According to a published account, the executives heard "top Bush administration officials talk about an upcoming rewrite of the federal Clean Air Act and the effect of energy policy on business interests." By the end of the week, the assembled guests had drafted a "Top Ten to-do list for Congress."

After leaving his government post, Smith managed the Washington office of an Oklahoma-based firm called Dunlap Codding & Rogers, to which, said his bio on the firm's website, he brought "a unique understanding of public policy and energy issues and how best to address them in the public and corporate arenas." He then became a senior adviser at the Abraham Group, an international consulting firm headed by Spencer Abraham, Bush's first secretary of energy. The Abraham Group is made up entirely of revolving-door alumni, particularly cronies of Abraham.

The list goes on and on.

"PORK-BARRELING" AS A LEGISLATIVE EPITHET IS A PRE–CIVIL WAR coinage that referred to the custom of handing out salt pork to slaves, who would crowd around the barrels that held it; and indeed, members of Congress have raided the federal treasury for home-district boondoggles ever since the earliest days of the Republic. By 1822, President James Monroe warned that financial support from Washington should henceforth be granted "to great national works only, since if it were unlimited it would be liable to abuse and might be productive of evil." The pork barrel was to become as central to our national political culture as the gerrymander or the filibuster; it has long been a foregone conclusion that whenever the federal government builds a road, or erects a dam, or constructs a power plant, members of Congress will artfully pad the bill with hometown "pork."

In the past two decades, though, the pastime has become breathtaking in its profligacy. Even as the federal deficit has soared to record heights, the sums of money being diverted from the treasury have grown ever larger. By 2005, 15,584 separate earmarks worth a combined $32.7 billion were attached to appropriations bills—more than twice the dollar amount in 2001, when 7,803 earmarks accounted for $15 billion, and more than three times the amount in 1998, when roughly 2,000 earmarks totaled $10.6 billion.

Congressman Dan Lungren of California returned to Congress in 2005 after a more than decade-long absence. "I'd walk down the hall and there would be streams of people in front of every office, representing every community and every public entity and every other special interest in that district—and they were all coming in for earmarks," he told Copley News Service during an interview that year. "We sure didn't have that when I was here before."

To be sure, not every project that receives an earmark is a waste of money. Such appropriations can fund after-school programs, park conservation, and public health. But huge sums of earmarked funds go for highly questionable purposes. As earmarking has proliferated, it has become less ad hoc and more efficient; it is now an accepted Washington industry, with its own standardized rules and procedures. Whereas in the past we had isolated thefts on behalf of constituents, what we have today is a professional crime syndicate with tentacles not only in long-established pork-barrel sectors such as public works and defense but in such relatively unspoiled fields as academic research and community programs. Those seeking government largesse no longer need to procure backroom meetings through congressional aides; most members of Congress now have simple "appropriations-request forms," which are as easy to complete as a typical job or credit card application.

By far the most significant change in recent years has been the incursion of lobbying firms, many of which have been set up for the express purpose of winning pork. Like attorneys at hospital bedsides, earmarking lobbyists aggressively court customers with boasts of their ability to deliver easy cash. "Shepherding appropriations requests through Congress is a priority for many clients," trumpets the website of B&D Sagamore, one such earmarking specialist. B&D's site furthermore promises to arrange "discussions between clients and members of Congress" and track legislation so that the firm can intervene "at critical points in the process."

By 2005, more than three thousand private companies or institutions had hired lobbying firms such as B&D to pursue earmarks. Because federal disclosure laws are so loose, it is difficult to estimate exactly how much money in total was doled out to lobbyists. But Keith Ashdown of Taxpayers for Common Sense, a Washington group that tracks the earmarking process, says the typical earmark seeker pays a retainer ranging from the tens of thousands up to more than a hundred thousand dollars per year, with the total easily reaching tens of millions of dollars. Large though that sum may seem, as investments, such retainers are undeniably savvy: the overall payout in pork is many times that, totaling into the billions.

For the aspiring pork recipient, mastering the appropriations process is hardly a difficult task. First, one needs simply to identify the correct member of Congress to approach with one's request. Almost always this will be a member whose district or state is home to the company or entity that will receive the money. Mark McIntyre, an appropriations lobbyist at the Russ Reid Company, wrote a 2003 how-to guide to appropriations for a Web publication called OnPhilanthropy, in which he said that lining up the best congressional "champion" often means the difference between success and failure. "It is extremely helpful," McIntyre pointedly noted, "if your U.S. Representative or one of your U.S. Senators serves on the Appropriations Committee."

Helpful indeed, as seen in the case of Ted Stevens, the senior senator from Alaska and chairman of the Senate Appropriations Committee from 1997 to 2004. A single mammoth bill in 2005 contained hundreds of earmarks for Alaska, including grants for projects on seafood waste ($160,000), salmon quality standards ($167,000), and alternative salmon products ($1.1 million, of which $443,000 was specifically set aside for the "development of baby food containing salmon"). Alaska's total haul came to $2,211.07 per capita, about twenty-two times the national average.

Mississippi, home of Senator Thad Cochran, who was first elected to Congress in 1972, also happens to be a leading recipient of appropriations bounty. Grants to his state in 2005 included $900,000 for "cattle and nutrient management in stream crossings," $248,000 for a study to prevent the spread of cogon grass, and $2.6 million for—the surest of sure bets—Mississippi State University's Thad Cochran Research, Technology and Economic Development Park.

Securing an earmark is never a given; only about one in four requests makes the final cut, and so steps must be taken to ensure that lawmakers are sufficiently stimulated. The most effective means is, of course, direct cash disbursements. As McIntyre forthrightly stated in his how-to guide, "Money has become the oxygen supply of political campaigns. For better or for worse, perhaps the best way to show your support for a Senator or Representative is to make a campaign contribution."

And yet direct contributions to lawmakers can get one only so far. Choosing the right lobbyist is as important as choosing the right lawmaker, if not more so. Because so many lobbyists have past experience on Capitol Hill, they know how to work the system and usually have personal ties to members and staffers who vet and prioritize the earmark requests. "You need to hire someone who understands the process and knows the pressure points," a Beltway lobbyist who specializes in winning appropriations money told me. "There's a lot of horse-trading going on, so you need someone who is hounding the staffers, calling up every week or every day if necessary."

Some lobbyists specialize in winning specific types of appropriations. If your seaside community wants taxpayers to foot the bill for having its beach restored, the man to see is Howard Marlowe. He has won dozens of such earmarks, mostly for already wealthy communities like Florida's Venice and New York's Fire Island. In late October 2001, on behalf of the American Shore & Beach Preservation Association, Marlowe's firm helped prepare a letter to Congress that bemoaned the economic toll that the events of September 11 had taken on the nation. "While these financial troubles pale in comparison with the unspeakable human losses of that day, they pose a significant problem," the letter went on. Urgent action was therefore required— specifically, lavishing money on beach communities in order to lure foreign and domestic tourists to America's shorelines. "Many national leaders have stated that increased tourism is imperative to the recovery of our economic strength," the letter claimed.

The defense appropriations bill is, as one might imagine, a

particularly popular target for seekers of pork. In 1980 there were just 62 earmarks in the defense appropriations bill; in 2005 there were 2,671, worth a combined $12.2 billion. That included $3 million to develop bathrooms made entirely of stainless steel; $3.75 million for alcoholism research (at, of all places, the Ernest Gallo Clinic and Research Center, in San Francisco); and $1 million to help eradicate brown tree snakes in Guam. It also contained $13.85 million for textile companies in North Carolina that produce clothing for the Pentagon, including Odor Signature Reduction Products for Special Forces and Smart Apparel for Warriors.

That latter line of clothing, subsidized with a million dollars in taxpayer money, is being developed by the Sara Lee Corp., which—though better known for its frozen cheesecakes, pies, and "brownie bites"—also has an apparel division based in Winston-Salem, North Carolina, that manufactures Playtex, L'eggs, and Wonderbra. I was never able to determine exactly what Smart Apparel for Warriors is, since no one at Sara Lee's headquarters in Chicago or in Winston-Salem was willing to talk about it; they claimed that the project, as a Pentagon contract, was too sensitive to discuss. But I was able to determine, through lobby disclosure forms, that the company obtained the money with the help (for a $20,000 retainer) of the well-connected PMA Group.

No immediate suspect emerged in the question of which member of Congress inserted Sara Lee's earmark. In the case of another winner in the defense earmarks sweepstakes, Night Vision Equipment Company of Allentown, Pennsylvania, there was not only a suspect but one with motive and means as well: Arlen Specter, a top Republican on the Senate Appropriations Committee.

Night Vision won a $1.25 million earmark in the 2005 defense bill, funding lobbied for by IKON Public Affairs, to which Night Vision paid $60,000. IKON deployed two lobbyists to work the Night Vision account, Peter Grollman and Craig Snyder, both of whom previously held senior posts on Specter's staff. Between 2000 and 2004, IKON donated $13,250 to Specter, with $7,250 of that coming directly from Snyder and Grollman. During that same period, Night Vision's then president, William Grube (along with his wife), kicked in $8,000 to Specter.

Just months before the defense appropriations bill passed, Snyder helped Specter fight off a fierce primary challenge from Pat Toomey. The electoral hopes of Toomey, who favored a ban on abortion, rested on his trouncing Specter in the state's conservative heartland, where the senator's pro-choice politics have made him a pariah. Shortly before the primary vote, Snyder put together a PAC called Pennsylvanians for Honest Politics, which promptly raised $17,750, with one third coming directly from Snyder and Grube.

Almost all of that money was spent to produce and air a radio ad that ran in the last few days of the campaign—on just a single Christian station that aired in primarily conservative areas. The ad savaged Toomey for failing to call, during an interview with Chris Matthews on *Hardball,* for criminal sanctions against a woman who gets an abortion. "Somebody who claims to be on our side had the opportunity to say abortion is murder," says the ad's protagonist. "Instead of showing the nation real pro-life leadership, Toomey shrunk like a frightened turtle." Specter won by just 17,146 votes out of more than a million ballots cast and did far better in conservative counties than expected.

Less than three months later it was Specter who announced that Night Vision had won the earmarks. "These projects, key to our nation's defense, will be invaluable in our continuing war against terror," he declared.

AFTER JACK ABRAMOFF COPPED A PLEA TO INFLUENCE-PEDDLING charges in early 2006, Republicans and Democrats in Congress promised that they would soon pass a tough new ethics reform package that curbed lobbyist abuses. Yet in June of that year, no such bill had yet been passed by the full Congress, and, as an Associated Press story put it, the "stench of scandal on Capitol Hill" was getting stronger every day. Even as Congress dawdled, the story noted, Congressman William Jefferson had yet to explain how $90,000 "in alleged bribery money ended up in his freezer"; Congressman Bob Ney of Ohio (who later went to jail) had come under criminal investigation for his ties to Abramoff; and Tom DeLay, who also was enmeshed in the Abramoff probe, had resigned in the face of allegations of election-related money laundering charges.

Meanwhile, several members of Congress had introduced, but failed to win approval for, at least six measures specifically targeting the foreign lobbying industry. One proposed new rule would have tightened restrictions on executive branch officials who left their jobs to become foreign lobbyists; another would have required members of Congress who retired and became lobbyists to wait at least five years before going to work on behalf of a foreign client.

Finally, in January 2007, the new Democratic-led House of Representatives—itself elected the previous fall in part due to disgust over congressional corruption—passed by a vote of 430 to 1 a package of reforms that aimed to limit the ability of lobbyists to curry favor with lawmakers. Soon afterward, the Senate approved an even tougher package (by 96 to 2), which was hailed by the watchdog group Public Citizen as "the most comprehensive lobbying reform" undertaken in many decades.

It remained to be seen whether the new rules would seriously impact the culture of influence peddling that pervaded Washington, but it was apparent from the outset that lobbyists representing foreign governments and businesses would not be greatly inconvenienced. That's because the changes approved by Congress had a more direct impact on those lobbying for U.S. corporations and other domestic clients. Whereas domestic lobbyists generally promote specific bills and legislation, the work of foreign lobbyists more frequently involves image management, much of which they seek to achieve through public relations campaigns targeting the media, think tanks, and the general public as much as Congress. If they are looking for federal money, foreign lobbyists don't go after congressional earmarks, but foreign aid from the State Department and financing for business ventures from agencies such as the Export-Import Bank. And none of the six measures that specifically targeted foreign lobbyists were included in the ethics reform bill passed by Congress.

That the new congressional rules did not more forcefully crack down on foreign lobbying was no small matter. For the ability of lobbyists to win favors in Washington for corrupt, dictatorial regimes is every bit as nefarious and detrimental to the health of our democracy as Jack Abramoff's winning influence with members of Congress through free meals and golfing trips, or Duke Cunningham's obtaining federal contracts for companies that bribed him with cash and prostitutes.

Lobbying for foreign countries and companies accounts for a relatively small component of the overall market, but it's a rapidly growing sector with vast revenues. I knew from my research that lobbyists working for particularly controversial clients were able to charge especially stiff fees—so firms willing to prettify a government as rotten as Turkmenistan's would be asking for serious money. Had I actually planned to hire a firm, coming up with the requisite dough might have been a source of concern. Under the circumstances, however, it meant that even if some lobbyists proved skittish about working with the Maldon Group, others would find the opportunity far too tempting to pass up.

FOUR

Strike a Pose:
Picking the Targets and Constructing a Cover Story

ORPORATIONS, NONPROFIT GROUPS, LABOR UNIONS, AND INDI-
viduals spend billions of dollars a year to retain Washington influence peddlers and PR specialists. As of
mid-2007, there were 1,862 foreign lobbyists registered with the
Justice Department, working for clients ranging from
Afghanistan to Zimbabwe. I'd settled on Turkmenistan as the
country-client, but still needed to pick the lobbying firms to be
approached. Given all of the options, how to choose which firms
would be offered the marvelous opportunity to help out the
Berdymukhamedov regime?

As much as possible, I wanted to make the story true to life
and hence illustrative of the everyday realities of Washington
lobbying. Approaching the right lobby shops was critical to the
pitch's credibility. So in making the selection, I established four

specific criteria. First, the firms picked would constitute a representative sampling of the high-end Washington lobbying community. I didn't want smaller bottom-feeders or fly-by-night operations that might be most expected to bite at any available business opportunity, no matter how sleazy.

Second, they should have an established record of employing sneaky practices, which would make it more interesting to expose their inside tricks. Third, they should have past experience working for controversial regimes. Last—since this still left quite a few lobby shops to pick from—they should be firms that had direct experience in the Caspian region. For example, Robert Cabelly, a former State Department and National Security Council official, had worked after retiring from the government as a lobbyist for African countries such as Angola, Equatorial Guinea, and Sudan (only briefly for Sudan, which the Bush administration had accused of committing genocide in Darfur—he was forced to ditch the contract after Congressman Frank Wolf of Virginia led a public campaign attacking him), so Cabelly would have been perfect if Chad's Deby regime had been the supposed client; but he made no sense at all to approach on behalf of Turkmenistan.

After speaking with friends and acquaintances that knew the foreign lobbying business well, I came up with a list of four firms to approach: APCO Worldwide, the Carmen Group, Cassidy & Associates, and the Livingston Group. (Why those four made the final cut will be explained shortly.)

Before contacting the firms, my personal and corporate cover stories still needed to be refined. The first few steps were easy. As a nom de guerre, I picked Kenneth Case, which seemed perfectly bland and inoffensive. Kenneth, of course, was my given name, and one I would be sure to respond to if addressed during a meeting (in the event I was able to set up in-person encounters at the lobby firms). I would be nervous enough going into meetings as it was; I didn't want to risk arousing suspicions by staring blankly if someone addressed me as "Jeremy," my initial choice. I picked the surname while listening to "Letter to an Occupant" by the New Pornographers, sung by the wonderful Neko Case.

Rafil Kroll-Zaidi, an associate editor at *Harper's,* designed a Kenneth Case/Maldon Group business card, which he produced on a printer at the magazine's New York office. We gave my company an address at a large office building in London, on Cavendish Square. I purchased a cell phone with a London number so I could allegedly make and receive calls from there while sitting in my home office in Washington. Rafil created a website for the Maldon Group and an e-mail account for Kenneth Case: case@themaldongroup.com.

Much of this was, in retrospect, recklessly thin and unlikely to withstand any serious scrutiny. My business cards were printed on flimsy cardboard stock, and looked far too cheap for an official from a fancy international energy firm like the Maldon Group. The website was merely a home page with our company address on Cavendish Square, and our phone number, preposterously, was the same as the one on my business card. Nor would it make any sense, if any of the lobbyists bothered to undertake even minimal due diligence, that our website was registered to a server located in Chesterton, Pennsylvania, a fact that could be discovered within seconds by anyone with even minimal knowledge of the Internet.

Even after these preparations, multiple problems abounded. Creating the Maldon Group allowed me to evade the impossibly doomed task of trying to pose as a Turkmen official and instead impersonate a Western businessman. It was a stretch, but with enough preparation I might be plausible in that role.

Yet I'd never even been anywhere near Turkmenistan. I knew nothing of local customs. I had no knowledge, beyond what was available through an Internet search, of Ashgabat, the capital. Kenneth Case would ostensibly have traveled at least a few times to that country, where the Maldon Group allegedly had huge investments at stake, and surely be minimally familiar with its capital city. Despite intensive coaching from a Russian-speaking friend, I couldn't even pronounce Berdymukhame-dov's name. And what would happen if I were asked for my impressions of Turkmenistan? Did Ashgabat have at least a few good restaurants? What was nightlife like? Friendly questions could easily trip me up, and there might be real trouble if any of the lobbyists I met had been to Turkmenistan. That seemed un-likely but hardly impossible, especially as all the firms I planned to contact had done business in the Caspian.

Hence, I further refined Kenneth Case's backstory, to make it consistent with his total ignorance of Turkmenistan.

The Maldon Group was based in London, but Case couldn't be British since I couldn't pull off that accent any better than I could a Turkmen one. So Kenneth Case, I determined, would be an American expatriate living in London. Life was funny, I'd say if asked (and I would be), but I'd more or less stumbled into my current position. I'd grown up in St. Louis, Missouri, and gone off to college in the Big Apple. While studying for a master's de-gree in political science at the New School for Social Research, I'd completed a semester's worth of courses in Rio de Janeiro. Growing disillusioned with academic work, I'd dropped out of the university and bummed around Brazil.

Up to this point, Kenneth Case's background actually mir-rored my own. Where we parted ways was that I'd ultimately re-turned to the States and embarked on a journalism career, whereas Case had remained in Brazil and—blame it on Rio—

fallen in love. Yes, my studies had been a bust but I'd met the lady of my dreams, a foreign graduate student from Lebanon. Her father lived in London and had heavy interests in international energy markets.

As I was aimless and without solid job prospects, he'd hired me (with an eye to his daughter's future) to be his general assistant and helper, whereupon I'd moved to London with my future bride. Even though I had no formal financial, business, or economics background, and didn't play much of a direct role in the energy business, I had put my nose to the grindstone and worked myself into the position of indispensable right-hand man. I set up meetings, arranged his schedule and travel, and generally made sure the trains ran on time. This cover story would explain, hopefully, why I knew not only nothing of Turkmenistan but virtually nothing either of the energy business, Caspian Basin trade, natural gas transportation, or pipeline networks.

My boss, I would further explain, had interests across the globe, among them the Maldon Group, of which he was a leading investor. I'd been temporarily assigned to the Maldon Group and—because I was originally from the States and knew Washington well—had been asked to set up and attend the initial round of exploratory meetings in the capital. Afterward, I would file a report for my boss and other investors. They alone would decide which of the firms to retain.

Even this cover story posed a number of obvious shortcomings. I'd been to London half a dozen times during the prior five years, but never for more than a few days. Any vetting of Kenneth Case, or even a screwup during the inevitable round of chitchat with the various lobbyists, could quickly reveal that I was not a city resident. I called a few friends in London and asked them for tips on how I might convincingly establish myself as a local, but never felt very comfortable. "I have a flat in Chelsea" was about the only line I could say with any conviction.

The plan seemed less than foolproof, but it would have to do.

In mid-February 2007, soon after Berdymukhamedov's ascent to power via the sham election, I began contacting the lobbying firms, by e-mail initially. I briefly introduced the Maldon Group and explained that we were eager to improve relations between the United States and the "newly-elected government of Turkmenistan." We required the services of a firm that could quickly produce a "strategic communications plan" and otherwise help us achieve our aims, which included arranging meetings between Turkmen government bigwigs and American officials at the State Department, in the National Security Council, and with Congress. I planned to be in Washington at the end of the month and hoped to set up meetings with a few firms that might be interested in handling the account. I wanted to discuss the type of services and strategies that the firms offered, an estimated budget, examples of previous work, and what sort of results could realistically be expected.

The first firm I contacted was APCO, via an e-mail to senior vice president Barry Schumacher, who was listed on the company's website as being responsible for bringing in new business. APCO had always been high on my list of lobby shops to offer the Turkmen deal. It had been voted "Agency of the Year 2006" by *PRWeek,* and its client list included a fair slice of the Fortune 500 (not to mention World Wrestling Entertainment, Inc., for which it helped, according to an APCO brochure I later received, "improve public perceptions and present a positive, responsible image to appeal to politicians, the media, parents, advertisers and the wider community").

APCO is also a leader in the field of "grassroots" lobbying.

During the 1990s, tobacco giant Philip Morris paid APCO more than a million dollars to create "grassroots" groups in all fifty states under the name of Citizens Against Lawsuit Abuse. The CALAs, as they were called, were designed to manufacture support for state and federal laws that would make it harder to bring lawsuits for injuries and illnesses caused by cigarettes and other hazardous products.

Section Review, a publication of the Massachusetts Bar Association, ran an article that detailed APCO's role in what it described as a massive campaign for lawsuit "reform" that was also secretly backed by insurance and chemical companies. It described the CALAs set up by APCO as sham "mouthpieces for anti-consumer tort law changes."

APCO was keenly aware of the need to keep its clients out of the limelight, as this would detract from the illusion that "tort reform" represented a spontaneous explosion by outraged citizens and small businesses. "You need to have credibility and that means when you pick people to join your coalition, make sure they're credible," Neil Cohen, an APCO executive who played a key role in setting up the CALAs, once said during an address to colleagues at a public relations conference. "And if they're not credible, keep 'em away. In a tort reform battle, if State Farm, [or] Nationwide, is the leader of the coalition, you're not going to pass the bill."

In Mississippi, APCO concocted Mississippians for a Fair Legal System for a "tort reform" campaign in 1993. During his address to colleagues, Cohen had chortled that weak disclosure laws meant that opponents "didn't really know [what business interests were] at the heart of everything" and that he had "fifteen hundred Mississippians mixed in with who our clients were."

More directly related to the project I had in mind, APCO had done recent PR work for the oil-rich, thuggish regime of Azerbaijan. Further back, in the mid-1990s, it had worked on behalf of the dictatorship of Sani Abacha, the Nigerian general who plundered billions of dollars from his nation's treasury and stashed it in Swiss bank accounts. Whether ruled by despot or (far more rarely) democrat, Nigeria historically has received plenty of support from American policymakers because it produces an extremely pure crude oil called "Bonney Light." One brochure produced by the Corporate Council on Africa, which promotes closer American ties with Nigeria, devoted an entire page to the superb qualities of Bonney Light, describing it as "highly sought after" and selling "at a premium on the spot market."

In the fall of 1995, APCO helped coordinate a visit to Nigeria by a delegation of African American newspaper publishers. In early October, after returning from their visit, the delegation held a press conference and announced that contrary to what had been reported by the world media, there was "no evidence of a dictatorship" in Nigeria. A press release APCO prepared noted optimistically that the delegation's visit coincided with "the much-anticipated . . . announcement by Chief of State Sani Abacha of democratic elections beginning in 1996."

A month after the press conference, Abacha's regime earned worldwide condemnation by hanging a well-known activist named Ken Saro-Wiwa and eight other democracy campaigners. No democratic elections were held in Nigeria under Abacha, who died while still holding power in 1998, of a heart attack he suffered while in the company of two prostitutes.

So it was no surprise that Barry Schumacher, after perusing the e-mail from the Maldon Group, wrote back to say he "would be delighted to put a team together" to meet Kenneth Case when he came to Washington. APCO, Schumacher continued in a follow-up note, "worked on image, policy, foreign investment and reputation issues for a host of governments," and noted that its "key professionals" included retired members of Congress and administration officials, specifically mentioning Elizabeth Jones, a former assistant secretary of state for Europe and Eurasia and ex-ambassador to Kazakhstan.

In another note I soon received, Schumacher asked if I might share a bit more information about the Maldon Group, since he hadn't (for obvious reasons) been able to discover anything about us. "I went on the web site (www.themaldongroup.com) and while a front screen came up, I could not access any information," he wrote. "Anything you can provide would be great."

I'd try to send a bit more info, I replied, but hinted that I wouldn't be able to add much. "We prefer to be discreet due to the sensitivity of our business," I wrote. Not to worry, Schumacher replied, offering that APCO would be "more than willing to sign a confidentiality agreement."

Emboldened by his craven attitude, I decided to push even further. A lawyer friend I consulted suggested that I reassure Schumacher about the Maldon Group's deep pockets and ability to honor our financial obligations, but to stonewall about our business operations. It was the former, he assured me, that Schumacher would be most concerned about. Hence, I fired off a fresh e-mail the following day (and subsequently sent a similar version to the other three firms that I spoke with). It read:

> After consulting with our counsel on your question involving the Maldon Group, I want to emphasize that discretion is the hallmark of our group's operations. If we were to proceed to the stage of contract negotiations, we'd certainly be able to satisfy any reasonable concerns about our ability to meet our obligations to you for services performed. Furthermore, any contract that we conclude would include a

reasonable and refreshable retainer as a key aspect. The firm with which we conclude a contract will receive much more detailed information (a confidentiality undertaking would be an essential part of any agreement) but we're not prepared to share much more than what I've already told you at the level of preliminary conversations. At this stage, we'd like primarily to discuss the changes underway in Turkmenistan and the possibility of putting together a communications strategy for the new government.

To which Schumacher promptly replied, "I understand, and this is not unusual for us." We soon confirmed a meeting, to be held at APCO's office in downtown Washington on the afternoon of February 27.

NEXT UP WAS THE CARMEN GROUP, WHICH WAS ALSO HAPPY TO MEET with the Maldon Group. However, Caleb Ward, an associate in the firm's international practice—to whose attention a receptionist had suggested I send an initial e-mail—wanted to speak directly with me "to learn a little more about what Turkmenistan wishes to accomplish with representation as well as more information about The Maldon Group." Via further e-mails, we set up a conference call for the following day in which Ward and two other members of the firm would participate: Steven Johnston, who had previously supported American investment in Eastern Europe at the Overseas Private Investment Corporation (OPIC), a U.S. government agency, and Michael Lempres, an executive managing director at the Carmen Group who served as the director of international affairs for the Department of Justice under George Bush the Elder and who, like Johnston, had previously worked at OPIC.

The Carmen Group had impressive ties to the Washington political establishment, particularly on the Republican side. Top figures at the lobby shop included Gerald Carmen, a former U.S. representative to the United Nations in Geneva under Ronald Reagan, and David Keene, chairman of the American Conservative Union and a former adviser to the presidential campaigns of Ronald Reagan, George H. W. Bush, and Bob Dole. The Carmen Group had an interesting track record on foreign lobbying as well. It had recently signed a $300,000 per year lobbying contract with the government of Algeria, for which it would promote congressional, public, and media support for "Algeria's legitimate interests and policy goals," according to papers filed with the Justice Department. The contract's terms required that Algeria pay for Carmen Group staffers to fly business class on international flights and be provided hotel accommodations equivalent to what the government provided for "high government officials and dignitaries."

What made the Carmen Group a logical choice for the Turkmenistan contract was past work the firm had done for Kazakhstan after James Giffen's P-Group had been disbanded. In 1999 and 2000, it received more than a million dollars from the government there to help establish President Nazarbayev "as one of the foremost emerging leaders of the New World." As further thanks, Nazarbayev gave Gerald Carmen, who handled the account, a tasseled cap and decorative whip, suggesting that he viewed the lobbyist as his personal trained monkey.

Carmen met with lawmakers on behalf of his client, and the firm paid for at least four writers—syndicated columnist Georgie Anne Geyer, *Providence Journal* associate editor Philip Terzian, R. Emmett Tyrrell, Jr., of *The American Spectator,* and Scott Hogenson of the Conservative News Service—to travel to Kazakhstan. All wrote articles that Carmen circulated on Capitol Hill and had published in Kazakhstan. None of the writers disclosed the source of funding for the trips, though Geyer and Hogenson noted that they traveled at the Kazakh government's invitation.

Geyer and Terzian visited in late 1999, when Kazakhstan was holding elections for the lower house of parliament. They wrote columns that criticized Nazarbayev but offered sympathetic—and at times upbeat—commentary. International observers found the elections substandard, Geyer wrote, but she deemed them a positive first step: "The elections looked good on the surface, and the government deserves credit for holding these first-ever elections for anything on a multiparty basis in Kazakhstan." This clashed with the U.S. State Department's assessment, which said the balloting "fell short of international standards" and that the regime had prohibited "some government opponents from running because they previously had been found guilty of political offenses such as publicly insulting the president."

Tyrrell and Hogenson traveled to Kazakhstan early the next year and filed enthusiastic dispatches. In an opinion piece published in *The Washington Times,* Tyrrell wrote that Kazakhstan "has at least four highly competitive political parties, . . . the freedoms of our Bill of Rights, and commendable tolerance."

This was just the sort of whitewash the Maldon Group was so desperately seeking for Turkmenistan, so I had high hopes when I phoned in at the agreed-upon hour for the conference call with the Carmen Group's team. While allegedly at my London office on Cavendish Square, I was actually in my home office wearing pajamas and sipping a cup of freshly brewed coffee. My chief fear as the conversation got started was that an ambulance, its distinctively non-British sirens squealing, would unexpectedly come barreling up the street in front of my house and raise questions about my whereabouts.

It quickly became clear that Johnston would be leading the discussion. Things got off to what seemed an auspicious start when he told me that the Carmen Group, if picked for the contract, would be willing to sign a nondisclosure agreement as I'd said would be required in an earlier e-mail to Ward. But Johnston had concerns about the Maldon Group and wanted to run a few things by me before we talked specifically about what sort of lobbying/PR campaign my firm envisioned for the Berdymukhamedov regime.

Among his questions, which I answered on the fly, were: How long had the Maldon Group been involved in Turkmenistan? ("A few years"); What type of firm were we? (Strictly investors, "we're not building plants or pipelines"); Was the company created for the specific purpose of the Turkmen project? (Yes); and Did we have any Russian investors? ("Yes, and a few Ukrainians as well"). That marked the end of the interrogation, but Johnston emphasized that at some point he would "want to have a frank and open discussion to assess whether we can help you. . . . The more information you can provide, the more helpful it would be."

I was unnerved. This was my first real interview with a lobbying firm, and I had been caught off guard by the aggressiveness of the questioning, especially after APCO's Schumacher had been so wonderfully accommodating in our e-mail exchanges. Fortunately, the tone warmed up considerably after that. Johnston told me that he had worked at the OPIC when he was in government, and that while there, he and Lempres together had insured a portion of a major energy pipeline that runs through the Caspian region. As a result, the Carmen Group was "pretty much on top" of issues like oil and gas transport, "the Soviet legacy," and regional politics. "Many firms are either Republican or Democrat," Johnston added, tossing in another of his firm's selling points. "We have both sides covered. We have a lot of contacts. We've helped local foreign embassies get the message out about reforms."

Lempres now chimed in, saying that the Carmen Group had roughly seventy employees, of whom nine were focused on international work. That team included former ambassadors and secretaries of state, and had a combined "twenty or so presidential appointments" among them. "We try to set measurable goals so after six months we can look back and see which ones we've hit," he said. "You want to be recognized for your role so if there's an improvement in the [bilateral] relationship—sometimes the improvement may not even have anything to do with our work—you can leverage that improvement for your own goals."

Johnston took over again, saying that the Carmen Group could arrange meetings with "a themed audience" for visiting Turkmen officials. "Anyone can get fifty people in a room if someone from the Ministry of Economy is coming here," he said. "We can get the right people in the room who want to hear what he has to say. . . . We could also identify a pool of investors and work to get the government's message to those investors."

The Carmen Group would also work directly on government-to-government relations, said Caleb Ward. For example, it might arrange a trade mission to Turkmenistan for American policymakers. For one foreign client, whom he didn't name, the firm had "created a congressional caucus to get people on the Hill to understand the issues and to build friendships."

The conversation continued for another few minutes. In the end, we set up a meeting for the following week when I would be "coming to Washington."

In firming up the details of that meeting, I sent Ward an e-mail to clarify where the Maldon Group's priorities lay. "Our broad goals . . . are centered on impacting the perception of

Turkmenistan in the media and political world, and generally improving political relations with the United States," I wrote. "I only mention this because we spent a fair amount of time yesterday talking about issues such as attracting trade and promoting investment. I . . . want to be clear that our agenda is on the political side, not the economic side."

Ward reassured me that his firm was up to the job. "The Carmen Group has extensive expertise in impacting perception in the media and political world as well as improving political relations between foreign countries and the United States," he replied. "We will of course evaluate what would be the best course of action to take after we have a chance to sit down with you and discuss matters further. We spent a fair amount of time yesterday talking about trade and investment mainly because it is something that many other firms in Washington do not offer to the level of expertise that Carmen Group does and since we assume that you are having ongoing discussions with other firms we wanted to distinguish ourselves."

I HAD BY NOW ALSO ESTABLISHED COMMUNICATIONS WITH CASSIDY & Associates, perhaps the most prominent of all Washington lobby shops. Between 1998 and 2006, Cassidy was paid some $235 million in lobbying fees, more than any other firm in Washington. I had asked many people for recommendations when I was deciding what firms the Maldon Group should offer the Turkmen deal to. There had been a wide range of opinion about the topic, but Cassidy's name came up time and time again. There just seemed to be something bloodlessly amoral about the firm that made it a top choice for just about everyone I asked.

Founded in 1970 by Gerald Cassidy, a former staffer for George McGovern, Cassidy & Associates had been known for much of its existence as a strongly Democratic firm. Cassidy pioneered the practice of lobbying for earmarks and also represented numerous Fortune 500 corporations as well as foreign countries and businesses. Its clients included Brigadier General Teodoro Obiang Nguema, who had ruled the small African nation of Equatorial Guinea since 1979, when he executed his uncle.

That seemed like a good idea at the time. The uncle, Francisco Macias Nguema, was a West African version of Idi Amin who banned opposition parties and in 1970 appointed himself "President for Life"—the first of a string of self-decreed titles that included "Leader of Steel," "Implacable Apostle of Freedom," and "The Sole Miracle of Equatorial Guinea." As many as fifty thousand people, roughly 10 percent of the population, were murdered during the Macias years—some were crucified along the road to the airport, for the benefit of visiting diplomats—and eighty thousand fled the country.

Obiang didn't kill as many of his citizens as Macias, but he managed to murder quite a few. He stamped out almost all opposition—he was last "elected" with 97 percent of the vote in 2002; the government or the president's relatives own the few media outlets in operation, and Obiang is widely deemed to be one of the world's most kleptocratic rulers.

Not even Gabriel García Márquez could have dreamed up Teodorín Nguema Obiang, the skirt-chasing, champagne-swilling, nightclub-hopping son of the president (and his potential successor). Teodorín holds a cabinet post—he's the Minister of Forestry, or the "Minister of Chopping Down Trees," as some call him—but very rarely attends government meetings. That's because he spends most of his time abroad: in Beverly Hills, where he lives lavishly, started a music company called TNO, and dated the rapper Eve, who had the good sense to dump him;

in New York City, where several years ago he offered $11 million to buy a Fifth Avenue condominium owned by Saudi arms dealer Adnan Khashoggi, only to be rebuffed by the condo's board; and in Paris, where he tools around in a white Rolls-Royce and a fleet of sports cars.

For a number of years, Cassidy had represented an Israeli firm called Merhav, which had significant interests in the Caspian, including Turkmenistan. Cassidy's deal with Merhav bore similarities to the arrangement I intended to float. A primary difference was that Merhav is a long-established, well-known international company, whereas the firm I created was a shady enterprise of murky origins and clearly suspect ethics. Furthermore, Cassidy's work for Merhav focused on promoting the Israeli firm's business interests in Turkmenistan and the broader Caspian region, including American financial support for a pipeline project. The Maldon Group's chief aim was to pretty up the Turkmen regime's image and win it friends in Washington.

I had exchanged a few e-mails with Gordon Speed, Cassidy's director of business development. He was very much the eager beaver, saying that he was "confident that we could help accomplish your goals with regard to improving bilateral relations between the U.S. and the newly-elected government of Turkmenistan," and proposing an introductory phone call with firm vice chairman Gregg Hartley.

Until 2003, Hartley had been a top aide to then House majority whip Roy Blunt. When he quit his Hill job and decided to become a lobbyist, a "bidding war for his services ensued," *The Washington Post* later reported. "Cassidy . . . won it with an offer of just under $1 million a year plus a substantial percentage of the lobbying fees paid by clients Hartley could bring to the firm." Hartley soon brought a number of new clients to Cassidy, "beginning with three of the former 'Baby Bell' telephone companies that were strong Blunt supporters: Bell South, SBC Communications (the two are now part of AT&T) and Verizon."

Hartley was known to have especially close ties to key Republicans in Congress. "Capitol Hill reporters take note," *The Hill* newspaper wrote in a story about Hartley soon after he left his job with Blunt. "The easiest, fastest way to get the cell and home phone numbers of top Republican staffers and lobbyists is to mention that you are writing a profile of Gregg Hartley. . . . Sources were beating a path to *The Hill*'s door to offer glowing reports." The newspaper said that a "pep squad of friends and former colleagues gave breathless descriptions" of Hartley, and had been so glowing in their praise that had they been allowed to go on "they may well have compared him to the late Mother Teresa." Hartley's hiring marked a key moment in Cassidy & Associates' transformation during the past decade into a lobbying enterprise that was increasingly identified with the Republican Party.

I expressed keen interest to Gordon Speed in speaking with Hartley, but warned about my ability to reveal very little, given the Maldon Group's concerns about discretion. "Fully understand," he promptly responded.

At 9:30 the following morning I rang Hartley's direct line, and his perky secretary put me right through. It turned out that this would be another conference call; Speed was with Hartley in his office, while Chuck Dolan, a PR guru who had served as a senior consultant for the Kerry-Edwards campaign in 2004, was patched in from Florida. The Cassidy team was far less probing than their counterparts at the Carmen Group, asking only a few softball questions about the Maldon Group.

Hartley asked me what my firm's goals were. Turkmenistan had a bad image, I replied, but things were changing with the election of the new president. Turkmenistan, I conceded, might not be a model democracy, but it was headed in the right direction. The new president—I never risked stating Berdymukhamedov's name directly, for fear of mangling the pronunciation—wanted to open up the economy and the political system, and we wanted to make sure he got a fair shake in the court of global opinion, especially in the United States.

Hartley was empathetic. He told me about his firm's work for Equatorial Guinea, which was "a very similar sort of representation to what you're talking about." Like Turkmenistan, the regime had major energy deposits, and it too had received some bad publicity. Hartley specifically mentioned a banking scandal involving the government, telling me that Cassidy's first job had been "to identify inaccurate or biased stories and try to correct them."

This was pretty amusing, since Hartley clearly had me in mind. A few years earlier, when working at the *Los Angeles Times*, I had broken the story of how Obiang had effective control over hundreds of millions of dollars in his country's oil revenues that were deposited at Riggs Bank in Washington. A Senate investigation not only confirmed the gist of what I'd reported, but uncovered even more dirt, such as the fact that Obiang and family members had stashed tens of millions of dollars in offshore accounts. These were the very same "inaccurate" stories that the good people at Cassidy had been working so hard to shoot down.

Hartley told me that for the past decade, Obiang had been on an annual list compiled by *Parade* magazine of what he dubbed the world's "most unacceptable rulers." I was familiar with the list—Hartley's term was a euphemism for what *Parade* more forthrightly and pithily called "dictators," but Hartley seemed unable to utter that word in referring to his client. "We now have him down to number eleven," Hartley boasted. "That may not sound like much, but it's something. There are a lot of international oil companies doing business over there and it makes it easier for them" when the public relations situation improves.

Though I didn't think it the right moment to say so, this progress for Equatorial Guinea did sound modest. And when I checked later, Obiang had in fact been deemed by *Parade* to be only the world's eleventh worst dictator, but in its brief summary the magazine noted that in 2003, "state radio announced that Obiang 'is in permanent contact with The Almighty' and that he 'can decide to kill without anyone calling him to account and without going to Hell.' " Referring to the Riggs scandal, *Parade* said, "Obiang himself told his citizenry that he felt compelled to take full control of the national treasury in order to prevent civil servants from being tempted to engage in corrupt practices. To avoid this corruption, Obiang deposited more than half a billion dollars into [offshore] accounts."

I told Hartley that I had read his biography on the firm's website, and while it was clear he had close ties to the GOP, I wondered whether his firm was also plugged in with Democrats. Absolutely, he said; in fact, firm founder Gerald Cassidy had worked on George McGovern's presidential campaign in 1972 and was still very close to Democrats, especially in the Senate. "We strongly believe in a bipartisan [approach] and mirroring the power structure," he said. "It's important to reach out to both sides—you have to find champions on both sides."

Chuck Dolan, who Hartley said would take the lead on "earned media and paid media" for Turkmenistan if Cassidy was retained, now stepped in. He'd spent eight years on the Advisory Commission on Public Diplomacy, which performs communications for the U.S. government overseas, and had done a lot of work in Eastern Europe. "Our approach would be to figure out your audience—journalists, obviously, but also think tanks and inside the Beltway publications," he said. "We can arrange meet-and-greets for Turkmen government officials, not only with their American counterparts but with think tanks and nongovern-mental organizations. They influence the influencers, and jour-nalists."

This all sounded great, but I reluctantly confessed that there was something that was troubling me. The Maldon Group really wanted to stay out of the limelight—wouldn't hiring a lobbyist for Turkmenistan expose us to unwanted scrutiny from the press? Hartley assured me there was little to worry about. True, public disclosure of the contract would be required, but "I'm talking a paragraph or two, not pages. . . . We're a discreet firm. We try to comply without conveying information that no one else needs to know. There are four or five firms that can handle this type of initiative and be successful. We think we're one of them."

Thirty minutes after the phone call started I had another meeting scheduled, this one for February 28 at 9:30 A.M.

THE LAST FIRM ON MY LIST WAS THE LIVINGSTON GROUP, WHICH WAS headed by retired congressman Bob Livingston of Louisiana. In 2007, *Washingtonian* ranked the capital's fifty most persuasive in-fluence peddlers. All but eight were former members of Con-gress, Capitol Hill staffers, administration officials, or Democratic or Republican party functionaries. At No. 8 on the *Washington-ian's* list was Livingston, who headed the House Appropriations Committee in the late 1990s before resigning from Congress in 1999. His unexpected departure, which occurred just as he was helping to spearhead the call for Bill Clinton's impeachment, became necessary when Livingston was forced to acknowledge that he himself had "on occasion" committed the sin of adultery. (Livingston's confession came after it became known that *Hustler* magazine was about to publish a story about some of those occasions.)

Livingston's disgrace proved to be short-lived: he immediately turned to lobbying and signed up a drove of clients. Among the first of these was a Louisiana firm called JRL Enterprises, which sought Livingston's help in winning earmarks for its "I CAN Learn" mathematics software. For JRL to have hired Livingston in the first place was a natural move: the year before he resigned, Livingston had slipped a $7.3 million grant into an appropriations bill for the then floundering firm. The earmark, the first JRL had ever received, provided it with virtually all of its income for 1998. After becoming a lobbyist, Livingston had received nearly a million dollars in fees from JRL, which, in turn, had received some $38 million in earmarks.

Yet there is very little (excluding JRL's own extravagant claims) to suggest that I CAN Learn significantly helps the learning of anyone at all. A 2005 story in the *Fort Worth Star-Telegram* found that students in the local school district, which has invested heavily in I CAN Learn, weren't learning math any more successfully than students elsewhere in the state. Meanwhile, local teachers complained that the software was freezing in the middle of lessons and sometimes provided the wrong answers to test questions.

The Livingston Group had also been effective for foreign clients, including Azerbaijan and Turkey. Its work for the latter has included general public relations, advocating for Ankara's right to purchase advanced American weaponry, and keeping Congress from declaring as genocide Turkey's massacre of more than one million Armenians during the early twentieth century.

In 2004, the House looked ready to pass a symbolic amendment on the question of Turkish responsibility for the genocide. Then Livingston's firm again sprang into action. "Its team also badgered everyone from top House aides to officials at the National Security Council, the State Department, the Pentagon, and Vice President Dick Cheney's office," *The New Republic* reported. "Against this onslaught, [the] amendment didn't stand a chance."

When I placed a cold call to the Livingston Group, the receptionist told me I needed to speak with James Pruitt, who before joining the firm had worked for Texaco and the American Petroleum Institute, and before that as Livingston's district representative in Louisiana. Since Pruitt was tied up in a meeting at the moment, she suggested I send him an e-mail with some general information. A few hours later, Pruitt replied, saying that "we would very much like the opportunity to discuss this in more detail" and that I would soon hear from him or another of the firm's senior officials.

The next day, the Livingston Group's Lauri Fitz-Pegado called me on my London cell phone (at my Washington home). Before becoming a lobbyist she had worked for the Democratic National Committee and as an assistant secretary at the Commerce Department during the Clinton years. Fitz-Pegado certainly had the sort of checkered past as a lobbyist that would have made her a natural PR flack for Turkmenistan. Her clients had included Haiti's notorious Jean-Claude "Baby Doc" Duvalier (when Fitz-Pegado was at Patton Boggs) and Citizens for a Free Kuwait, a front group funded almost entirely by the government of Kuwait to promote the 1991 U.S. war in the Persian Gulf (while she was employed at Hill & Knowlton).

Fitz-Pegado's grandest achievement for the latter was to help set up the congressional testimony of a fifteen-year-old Kuwaiti girl—known only by her first name of Nayirah, allegedly for the protection of her and her family, who might be subject to Iraqi reprisals in occupied Kuwait—who tearfully told of how she had personally witnessed Iraqi soldiers enter a hospital in Kuwait and take babies out of incubators. "I volunteered at the al-Addan hospital," said Nayirah's moving testimony, which was distributed in a press kit prepared by Hill & Knowlton. "While I was there, I saw Iraqi soldiers come into the hospital with guns, and go in the room where . . . babies were in incubators. They took the babies out of the incubators . . . and left the babies on the cold floor to die."

The story, which provoked a spate of political and media outrage that led to a drumbeat of support for war, subsequently proved to be bogus. Nayirah, it emerged, was a member of the Kuwaiti royal family and had been coached in her false testimony. The Kuwaiti government funneled roughly $12 million to Citizens for a Free Kuwait, of which about $11 million was paid to Fitz-Pegado's firm in the form of fees.

Fitz-Pegado opened the conversation by asking a few general questions about my firm and me, saying she wanted "to see if there's a synergy." I gave the usual vague replies. We were a group of private investors, whom I couldn't identify. Nor was I able to say much about the Maldon Group's corporate structure, as that was "above my pay grade."

Fitz-Pegado also expressed interest in how I'd come to contact her firm. I told her the Maldon Group had a few associates in the United States who had helped compile a list of firms with experience in the Caspian, and that furthermore we'd heard very good things about the Livingston Group through the grapevine. "Oh, so you're speaking with other groups as well?" she asked. I conceded we were.

Now I asked her to describe the assets the Livingston Group would bring to the table for Turkmenistan. She reeled off a few past and present clients, including Turkey, Azerbaijan, Morocco, Congo, and the Cayman Islands, and said the firm's top-notch staff and affiliated consultants included six former members of Congress, evenly divided between Democrats and Republicans, as well as a former communications director for the National Security Council and a deputy spokeswoman at the State Department. Fitz-Pegado herself had been "doing this since 1982" and had represented about twenty-five foreign governments. "We welcome opportunities like this where we think we might be able to make a difference," she said. "We can combine bipartisan access on Capitol Hill, a strong relationship with the current administration—it's going to be in power for another two years, so you need that—and a relationship with think tanks and policy institutes that can influence the debate and the media."

Fitz-Pegado told me that the Livingston Group had developed congressional caucuses for other clients, including Turkey, where "we got certain members of Congress to quote unquote sign up, to be advocates on the Hill." She suggested that the firm could put together a target list of meetings for Turkmen officials coming to Washington. "A lot of firms are retained for huge sums of money and at the end of the day the client says, 'What did you do for me?' " she told me. "I believe in delivering for the client—the deliverables could be that the ambassador doesn't know anyone in Congress and wants to meet fifty members. As you talk to other firms, whether we are the firm you go with or not, you want to talk about deliverables."

How much information would we need to make public if we hired the Livingston Group? I asked. Fitz-Pegado said she could do a legal check after knowing more about what exactly we wanted her firm to do. "If you're traipsing around with us and the foreign minister, you should be prepared for some disclosure," she said, but assured me the information we would need to provide would likely be minimal.

Well, I said, I'd definitely like to meet with the Livingston Group when I came to town. I knew it was short notice but I hoped they'd be able to squeeze me in. "Sure," replied Fitz-Pegado. "We do this all the time." Unfortunately, Bob Livingston would be away during my trip to Washington, but other key people would be available. We'd confirm the date and time for the meeting over the next few days.

Fitz-Pegado soon e-mailed with details for a proposed meeting date "with a senior level team" and to say that the "standard fee structures for the scope of work we discussed yesterday" would be about $40,000 per month. But a chill had crept into her previously friendly tone. Prior to the meeting, she suggested, both sides should "sign a nondisclosure agreement which would allow us to learn more about your company." She and Pruitt subsequently e-mailed with questions about the Maldon Group. Pruitt wanted to know if any Turkmen officials had "an equity or any other financial interest in your company." Fitz-Pegado asked for the name of my Lebanese boss—which I'd pointedly refused to disclose to any of the firms I spoke with, partly because he didn't exist, and partly because though I could have made a name up, I wanted to be as secretive as possible—and about the ownership structure of the Maldon Group.

I'd always worried about being exposed as a fraud during the personal meetings, and my intent all along had been to set up meetings, if possible, with four firms but only go ahead with appointments at two. More face time than that seemed needlessly risky. The decision on which two to meet directly with would be based on due diligence, or more precisely which firms did the least due diligence in their initial assessments of Kenneth Case and the Maldon Group. The Livingston Group's questions didn't seem that hard to handle—and, particularly given the promise of confidentiality, would have posed no problem if the Maldon Group actually existed—but Pruitt and Fitz-Pegado had annoyed me with their requests for information. Furthermore, I couldn't possibly sign a nondisclosure agreement, as that would legally prevent me from reporting on my contacts with the Livingston Group.

I waited a few days and then e-mailed Fitz-Pegado to cancel our meeting, saying only that the Maldon Group would be taking "another route." To her credit, she didn't seem sorry to see me go, sending a polite but brief note in reply wishing us the "best of luck."

The Carmen Group had also put me off, particularly Johnston's requests for additional data about the Maldon Group. I didn't have to stand for that, especially since APCO and Cassidy & Associates had proved to be such total patsies. So I canceled my meeting there as well. "Though I am sorry to hear that you have decided to go in a different direction I wish you luck in your work with Turkmenistan," Ward e-mailed by way of reply. Like Fitz-Pegado, Ward didn't try to talk me out of my decision to drop his firm as a potential hire, though he did urge me to get back in touch in the future if we changed our minds.

I had a week before my scheduled meetings with APCO and Cassidy, and there were still a few details to be ironed out. First, lobbying experts I consulted with had told me that the Maldon Group would never send Kenneth Case alone to Washington; to enhance my credibility I should bring along a phony colleague. I'd made calls to friends and associates to see if anyone would be willing to accompany me to the meetings, but initially found no takers.

Then I remembered a friend who would be perfect for the task. Irene was a young, attractive Russian, which made her just about perfect to play the part of my colleague. She didn't know anything of the Eastern European gas trade, but she wouldn't have to do much at the meeting other than listen attentively, take notes, pronounce Berdymukhamedov's name, and perhaps periodically mutter a few words in Russian. Irene found the chance to be an actress hugely amusing and instantly agreed to join me. I'd mentioned in my e-mails and conversations with the lobbyists that I'd be bringing a colleague along with me to the Washington meetings—Irene Shostakovich, I'd said, picking the surname of one of the most famous and widely performed composers of the twentieth century, from the Maldon Group's Moscow office.

But now, when I went to Irene's home a few days before the first date at APCO to finalize matters, she was panic-stricken. "I can't do it," she said. "I'm afraid I might say something stupid and blow the whole thing for you." I tried to buck up her confidence, but she refused to reconsider; it looked as though there would be no colleague joining me for the meetings.

However, luck was with me. Irene's husband, a forty-nine-year-old Spaniard named Ricardo, had sat in on our conversation. When she backed out, he said he'd be happy to come along. My initial instinct was that I'd be better off without him. Irene was always neat, proper, and well dressed; like me, Ricardo invariably wore jeans and sneakers, and I couldn't imagine him playing the part of an international businessman. But when I mentioned this, Ricardo went to a closet and pulled out a number of expensive, fashionable business suits. To my great surprise, Ricardo had studied economics at the university level and had been involved in the import-export trade some years earlier. He'd even been involved in negotiating energy deals in the Middle East.

With his background, Ricardo could converse easily about

topics like foreign direct investment and structuring energy deals. Even better, he had a sly, roguish appearance. He looked like a guy who would be adept at fulfilling just the type of tasks that a sleazy firm seeking favors in Turkmenistan would find helpful—say, lining up a prostitute for a visiting oilman or routing payments to a government official's offshore account.

I contacted Rafil at *Harper's* the next day and he immediately printed up and shipped me business cards for Ricardo, and created an e-mail account for my firm's new consultant as well. The cell phone number we printed on his cards was off by a digit from mine. It was for a nonworking number in London, but I'd be taking the lead at the meetings with APCO and Cassidy, and we'd just have to hope that none of the lobbyists would decide to call him.

There were a few final items to deal with before the meetings, especially taking steps to ensure that the sting not be exposed. It would be bad enough if the lobbying firms wised up at some point over the coming months, before *Harper's* had published the story, which could put the whole project at risk. But my nightmare scenario was being identified as a journalist while on the premises of one of the lobbying firms. Police involvement was unlikely—though in my most paranoid moments I could envision myself in handcuffs, trying to shield my face from a *Washington Post* photographer as the cops led me away—but being busted on-site would have been a personal and professional humiliation. The lobbyists would have gone straight to the press, and the whole debacle would surely have been covered. I wouldn't mind being hammered by the lobbyists for using undercover tactics if I came away with a good story; but the prospect of not getting a story and being ridiculed as an incompetent boob was terrifying.

Washington is fundamentally a small town, and there was a

possibility, however remote, that someone at one of the firms might recognize me from an event around town or from a TV news appearance. Since I'd written about both firms and their clients in the past, and had been one of the few American journalists to regularly cover Equatorial Guinea, it also seemed possible that a lobbyist at APCO or Cassidy might have seen my picture while conducting opposition research. Maybe I was being paranoid, but disguising my appearance seemed like a smart precaution and surely couldn't hurt.

I turned for help to a friend who had worked undercover for the CIA. Nothing dramatic was needed, he said, since no one I was going to meet knew me well. All I needed to do was take a few simple steps in the event that I looked vaguely familiar to one of the lobbyists, and dampen down any glimmer of recognition that might be sparked. He told me that one strong identifier, even if subconscious, was the shape of a person's face. Based on his advice, I trimmed and narrowed my full beard, leaving only a chin curtain, and had my hair cropped short. I dyed my normally salt-and-pepper hair (and beard) jet black and applied gobs of mousse to emulate the look of a European yuppie. And I bought a pair of large, round glasses with clear lenses.

I owned several suits, but none good enough for Kenneth Case, the right-hand man of a major international energy investor. Two days before my meeting with APCO, I purchased an expensive dark business suit and a light blue shirt and tie. A friend lent me his fancy business briefcase. Rafil, my accomplice at *Harper's* in New York, had even shipped me a fake Cartier watch he asked an acquaintance to buy in Hong Kong.

Last, I went to RadioShack and bought a small digital recorder so I could tape the meetings at APCO and Cassidy. I had weighed the pros and cons of taping for some time, and decided in favor for several reasons. Some years earlier I had done an undercover piece for *Mother Jones* magazine, during which I'd flown to the Bahamas posing as a rich American investor with vast wealth of dubious origins, and very quickly opened up an offshore account. The article was meant to draw attention to the growing scourge of money laundering, whereby rich individuals and companies have transferred trillions of dollars to offshore financial havens, beyond the reach of tax and law enforcement authorities (not to mention angry ex-spouses and creditors).

While in the Bahamas I'd spent a good deal of time with an official from a law firm in Nassau, who'd generously helped navigate me through the world of Bahamian banking. "You've done just the right thing," he'd told me. "If you're going to put your money away, you want to make sure it's in good hands. And this is a very good, safe place to put your money." After the piece was published in *Mother Jones,* the official insisted he'd never met me. The Associated Press, which wrote an article about my story, credulously reported his denial. I thought it unlikely, given the e-mails I already had in hand and more evidence I would likely receive at the meetings, that the lobbyists would flat-out deny having met me. But I expected that they would claim that I'd taken things out of context or seek to minimize their actions in one way or another. I wanted irrefutable proof to rebut them if that were to become necessary.

Second, I consulted with an attorney who, though not familiar with state-by-state laws on secret recordings, advised me to record the conversations with lobbyists in order to ensure that I got the most accurate possible account of the meetings. He believed that whatever the relevant general law on taping conversations, my use in this instance would withstand legal challenge if the recording were made strictly to enhance my reporting and ensure its accuracy. If NBC's *Dateline* could use hidden cameras for its "To Catch a Predator" series, he said, there was no way that it could be illegal to secretly tape lobbyists hoping to represent Turkmenistan.

And it turned out that taping the meetings would be legal, since the meetings would be held in Washington. A state-by-state guide on the website of the Reporters Committee for Freedom of the Press says, "Thirty-eight states and the District of Columbia permit individuals to record conversations to which they are a party without informing the other parties that they are doing so. These laws are referred to as 'one-party consent' statutes, and as long as you are a party to the conversation, it is legal for you to record it."

So I was all set to go. In order to feel slightly more comfortable in my getup, I went for a short stroll in my neighborhood on the afternoon before the meeting, in full regalia. As I was returning home I walked by a neighbor who'd known me casually for the past decade. I looked him in the eye as I passed.

He never blinked. I was a perfect stranger.

FIVE

T HE MALDON GROUP'S MEETING WITH APCO WAS SCHEDULED FOR three o'clock on February 27, and I had a hard time concentrating that morning. After pacing about my home office and aimlessly surfing the Web for hours, I put on my new business suit and glasses and waited for Ricardo to drop by for our previously arranged last-minute consultation. The doorbell rang in the early afternoon. As he'd promised, Ricardo had done an impressive job of transforming himself from casual slacker into international businessman. He wore a dark Hugo Boss suit with a dapper blue pastel tie, topped with a stylish wool overcoat. The only thing that worried me was a leather-bound but cheap-looking writing pad he was carrying, which we decided he should leave behind.

Ricardo and I had already agreed that I'd carry the conversation at the meeting with APCO; he would only interject if I was faltering or if he felt especially comfortable discoursing about a particular topic. Ricardo in many ways was better suited than I for a meeting with Beltway lobbyists, but the more he talked, the more likely it would be that we'd trip each other up with conflicting statements. Furthermore, no matter how vague and innocuous his remarks, they might not jibe with my own past statements and e-mail exchanges with Schumacher. Just having Ricardo along made me far more relaxed, though, in part because he seemed thoroughly unruffled about playing his role. And if things went badly, especially if in a worst-case scenario our cover was blown, it was a huge comfort to know that I'd have a companion with whom to beat a hasty retreat.

Did APCO smell a rat? Would we be vetted upon arrival? There was no telling, so to be on the safe side Ricardo and I patched together a story about our visit to Washington. Our story, as concocted at my dining room table, was that we'd arrived in town a day earlier, he from Madrid and me from London. We'd be meeting with three other firms, though of course we couldn't identify precisely who the competition was. We even picked a place where we were lodged, so we wouldn't look blankly at each other or blurt out two different answers if that came up during casual banter. We settled on the Mayflower Hotel, on Connecticut Avenue not far from the White House, as our local headquarters.

My house is in Washington's Mount Pleasant district, a few miles north of APCO's downtown offices. It was a cool but mild winter afternoon, and we walked the few blocks to Sixteenth Street, where we flagged a cab. Even Ricardo was a bit edgy when we arrived at APCO's building near the intersection of Twelfth and H streets NW—I'd started the recorder and placed it in my inside jacket pocket a few minutes beforehand—and things got off to an inauspicious start. The lobby security guard, a real pit bull, demanded to see ID other than our Maldon Group business cards before letting us take the elevator upstairs to APCO's fourth-floor office. Ricardo flashed his Washington, D.C., driver's license and wrote down his name on a sign-in sheet. That seemed fine, as he wasn't using a pseudonym, but I had already shown the guard my business card with the name of Kenneth Case. She might not notice that my driver's license had a different name, but I had no intention of signing in under my real name regardless.

I still wasn't sure whether APCO had any suspicions about my bogus company and me, but if for any reason someone from APCO were to take a look at the building sign-in logs, the name Ken Silverstein below Ricardo's would trigger alarm bells. A follow-up Google search would be fatal.

I argued with the security guard, telling her I'd forgotten my overcoat at the hotel; my wallet was in the pocket. She was unmoved and phoned up to APCO. A few minutes later a cheerful Barry Schumacher came down to get us. I introduced Ricardo and apologized for the screwup. He said not to worry about it, resolved the problem with the security guard, and escorted us to a bank of elevators. On the way up to APCO's office, Schumacher carried on an animated conversation in Spanish with Ricardo.

We exited the elevator on the fourth floor and Schumacher led us into APCO's suite and straight into a conference room, just past the reception area. As we entered the room, three of Schumacher's colleagues rose from their seats around the conference table to greet Ricardo and me.

First up was Elizabeth Jones, the former assistant secretary of state and ex–ambassador to Kazakhstan whom Schumacher had mentioned in his original e-mail to me. Jones's résumé was indeed impressive. With thirty-five years in the Foreign Service, she had attained the rank of career ambassador and had government experience in Asia, the Middle East, and Europe.

Next came Robert Downen, a professorial type in a casual dress shirt and tie who had previously served as a senior aide to Senator Robert Dole, as a fellow at the Center for Strategic and International Studies, and before that as an adviser to Paul Wolfowitz when the latter served as assistant secretary of state during the Reagan years. (At the time of the meeting, Wolfowitz was the number two official at the Pentagon.)

Last, in a pin-striped suit, was Jennifer Millerwise Dyck, who Schumacher told me by way of introduction (and as I already knew well) had formerly been the chief spokeswoman for Vice President Dick Cheney. She ran press operations in seventeen states for Bush-Cheney '04, according to her biography that I received that day, and "regularly represented the campaign in television and radio appearances." After that, she'd handled communications at the CIA, where she'd "initiated the agency's first coordinated corporate branding and advertising strategy." She'd left that job only recently and come to work for APCO.

In fact, I'd spoken with Dyck many times in the past in the course of reporting stories on the CIA, but this was the first time, thankfully, that I'd met her in person. I'd heard on the news earlier in the day that there'd been a bombing in Afghanistan during a visit there by Cheney. "You're probably glad you're not with him today," I said. Dyck joked that the vice president had received a lot of criticism in the press—she mentioned the "hunting accident," a reference to the incident in which Cheney had accidentally shot a friend in the face while quail hunting—but said that all of his PR problems postdated her time as his spokeswoman.

After the introductions, everyone took a seat at the table. The room was bland and sparsely decorated. A coffeepot and a black plastic tray of cookies lay on a countertop across from where I sat. Schumacher, having taken off his jacket and placed it over his chair, offered Ricardo and me refreshments, which we both declined.

It became apparent quickly that APCO had swallowed the cover story and didn't plan to challenge us, politely or otherwise, with questions designed to establish our bona fides. Schumacher did ask if we wanted to further summarize our goals, but I said there wasn't much to add at the moment: we wanted to hire a firm that could promote the Turkmen government, which would strengthen our own position in the country. I wasn't going to pretend that there was a "perfect situation" in Turkmenistan, but the new government wanted to improve its relationship with the United States and the Maldon Group wanted to do its part to help. Ricardo and I would be holding additional meetings with contenders for the contract over the next few days. We'd file a report with our superiors after we returned to London, and they'd settle on the firm they preferred to work with. The next step would be to bring over a few of the Maldon Group's big investors to meet with the winning lobbying team in Washington, or alternatively fly the lobbyists to London on our corporate jet for a meeting there.

When I made it clear that no additional information would be forthcoming, Schumacher handed out a few items to Ricardo and me: a thick corporate brochure about APCO; a thirty-one-page bound notebook of color slides from a PowerPoint presentation titled "A Communications Program for Turkmenistan in the United States," whose cover page featured the red, green, and white Turkmen flag with stars and a crescent moon; and a CD-ROM of the presentation that we could take back to London. "We can just have a casual conversation, or we can show you the presentation," Schumacher said. It seemed far safer to be a passive observer than an active participant in the meeting, so I immediately asked that they run through the PowerPoint.

Schumacher fired up the slide show, which he projected onto a wall screen, where all eyes swiveled. He started by laying out what "sets APCO apart" from any competitors we were considering. The first slides covered information about the firm and some of its recent successes. APCO had been founded in 1984 with "one person and one office," but now had $73 million in revenues and a "client satisfaction" rate of 98 percent (an approval rate almost as high as the Turkmenbashi had racked up in his electoral triumphs). The firm had hundreds of corporate clients, including seven of the top ten companies on Fortune's Global 500. Among its satisfied customers were Microsoft, Boeing, Harrah's Entertainment, and Altria, which APCO represented back in the day when that company was still called Philip Morris.

APCO had worked for more than twenty-five different governments on "reputation management," "investment promotion," and "advocacy and policy change." Two slides flashed onscreen showing the flags of past clients, including Kazakhstan ("We arranged high-level visits for leading officials"), Mongolia ("APCO worked with the U.S. government to get [it] certified" for an economic aid program), and Turkey ("for whom we have increased congressional support" and "defeated legislation harmful to it").

Schumacher stopped here to highlight APCO's work on behalf of Romania in the 1990s, when the government found itself in a situation "exactly analogous to where Turkmenistan is now." APCO had been hired not long after the fall of Nicolae Ceauşescu, one of the most brutal of the old Communist rulers in Eastern Europe. Ceauşescu was overthrown by a coup in 1989; he and his wife, Elena, fled the capital by helicopter but were captured by the army. The couple were hastily tried and executed by firing squad on Christmas Day. That put an end to lobbyist Edward von Kloberg's contract with the Ceauşescu regime, but his bad fortune ultimately redounded to APCO's benefit. "When we were hired there were a lot of questions about what the new government was going to do, about the influence of the old apparatchiks, about whether they were really going to establish a democracy," Schumacher said. "It was a situation where the new government had a bad reputation. . . . They had no friends in Congress, trade was very low with the United States, and they had no business allies."

Despite that, APCO had worked wonders for the post-Ceauşescu government. Three months before the firm was hired, Congress had voted unanimously against extending Most Favored Nation trade status (MFN) to Romania. "We did some public advocacy work, worked with the embassy, identified firms with investments or who wanted to invest, and built a coalition," Schumacher said with an air of satisfaction. "We were able to get MFN passed, which was the government's top priority."

Yes, the parallels with Turkmenistan were readily apparent, I thought to myself, but there were some notable differences as well. In the case of Romania, the dictator had been executed and a revolution had swept aside the old order. A controversial government had taken its place, but it had popular support and did not have a ghastly and lengthy paper trail of human rights violations. In the case of Turkmenistan, the dictator had died while he still held power and the old regime lived on in the person of Berdymukhamedov, the Turkmenbashi's trusted former associate, dentist, and henchman.

Another early slide was called "Soft Soundings," and it ran through what Schumacher described as a "vox populi of policymakers" on the subject of Turkmenistan, gleaned from interviews conducted by him and his colleagues in preparing for the meeting with the Maldon Group. Now is "Turkmenistan's most important moment since independence," read one quote, attributed to an unnamed foundation fellow. "The Great Game is being played out in Ashgabat," said a second sounding, which significantly overstated Turkmenistan's role in the Caspian Basin energy game, but was heartening nonetheless. "No one is looking for perfection on democracy and human rights reforms," read another sounding, this one from an administration official. I wagged my head, encouraged by the welcome news contained in this latter sound bite. "This really is an opportunity to define the new government of Turkmenistan," Schumacher said.

Several other slides deepened the "Situation Analysis" APCO had prepared on Turkmenistan, and it seemed there was good news on just about every front. The Bush administration, Schumacher read along with one slide, was "ready to focus on Turkmenistan" and offer support on "energy and other issues." The U.S. government was "realistic" about the situation, and would be satisfied with "some modest, concrete results" on issues such as Internet access and student exchanges.

APCO reported that Congress was watching events in the country with heightened, even keen, interest. The new Democratic majority wanted to "help craft foreign policy in the region," and lawmakers were seeking "ways to advocate for American interests separate from the fight against terror." With its hefty energy reserves, Turkmenistan had a role to play. This was another exaggeration of Turkmenistan's alleged importance to the future well-being of the United States. In fact, just a few slides earlier, an anonymous congressional staffer was quoted in the "Vox Populi" section as saying—far more accurately, one suspects— "There are only about ten members of Congress who could find Turkmenistan on a map."

But the point now was that there was "a short window of op-

portunity" for Turkmenistan "to redefine and promote itself."
The Berdymukhamedov regime needed to "act fast to take advantage" of the situation. The message couldn't have been
clearer: Turkmenistan needed to hire APCO, and now. Otherwise, the chance to end the country's isolation—and incidentally, fatten APCO's bottom line—would be squandered, and the
window of opportunity would slam shut.

Elizabeth Jones stepped in. After speaking with her former
colleagues at the State Department and other agencies, she said,
she had concluded that the Bush administration was hoping to
improve relations with the Berdymukhamedov government.
Her contacts at State weren't expecting "miracles" or "an over-
night change" in terms of political reform; even a few small
steps would provide some "good hooks" APCO could use to promote the regime.

This reminded Schumacher of something else that set APCO
apart from its competitors: high-level former officials like Jones,
a class act who was willing to "roll up her sleeves" and phone old
colleagues on behalf of her clients. "People like Beth can call up
these policymakers," Schumacher said with a shake of the head,
as if he himself were in awe of Jones's access. "Getting information like that with a couple of phone calls is priceless."

Schumacher himself was no slouch either, though he was
too modest to boast about it. He did allow, however, that he had
made a few strategic calls of his own and had learned from a
staff director at "a key committee" that hearings on the topic of
energy security were coming up. "Turkmenistan has a role to
play here," he said. "That helps us talk about Turkmenistan in a
positive way."

In addition to the core team around the table, Schumacher
emphasized that APCO had on staff a number of other heavy-
weight Washington players that could be called on if needed on

an ad hoc basis. The firm's roster, one slide revealed, included 10 ex-ambassadors, 17 former elected politicians, 41 retired government officials, and 90 former political advisers. APCO executives who might be especially useful included former Michigan senator Don Riegle, who, Schumacher said, was tight with Senate majority leader Harry Reid, and former congressman Don Bonker, who he said had close ties with Tom Lantos, the new Democratic chairman of the House Foreign Affairs Committee.

This was an impressive duo all right, and in more ways than one. Before becoming a lobbyist, Riegle had been chairman of the Senate Banking Committee and became known as one of the "Keating Five," the group of senators who had taken huge donations from savings and loan swindler Charles Keating and intervened on his behalf. So egregious were Riegle's efforts on behalf of Keating that he'd been admonished by the Senate ethics committee—a rare rebuke from a body that a friend of mine once described as the "Member Protection Committee."

As for Bonker, I had met him several times back in the 1980s when I was a student at the Evergreen State College in Olympia, Washington, and he was in Congress. Even then it was clear that he had the principles of a marshmallow. At liberal Evergreen he'd come and give a speech that was so fervent in his opposition to American intervention in Central America that he'd come across like Che Guevara; then a few days later there'd be a newspaper account of a talk he'd given to a conservative group in which he sounded like Ronald Reagan Lite.

Riegle and Bonker had ties to the Democrats, but what about the Republican side? I asked with concern. Schumacher assured me that the firm had access to people in both parties, "not because we've contributed money," but because of the high esteem in which the firm's stable of former officials was generally held. (Though, as I subsequently discovered, APCO employees had contributed a modest but notable $100,000 during the last three election cycles. Bonker had contributed $4,500 of that amount to Lantos, including, coincidentally, a $1,000 contribution two days after my meeting with APCO.)

APCO's staff included a number of former top Republicans, including Richard Allen, a former national security adviser under Ronald Reagan, and Scott Milburn, who had worked as a White House budget spokesman for the Bush administration. And, Schumacher added with a grin, Dyck had extremely strong ties to the GOP; she alone was "worth" six of APCO's Democratic lobbyists.

"What can I say?" Dyck crowed, throwing her arms out.

I also delicately asked about the quality of APCO's congressional contacts. The firm, I inquired, worked with a number of senior members, not just low-level flunkies, right? Absolutely, said Schumacher, but APCO was always looking to identify congressional "up-and-comers" as well. That allowed the firm to "cultivate a serious relationship so in a few years, after they've risen through the ranks, you have a friend and ally."

Before long, we came to an important slide labeled "Budget Parameters," which revealed the proposed cost for APCO's Turkmenistan operation: $40,000 per month, plus "reasonable and normal" expenses, which were estimated at about ten percent of fees, or another $4,000 monthly. That didn't include travel outside Washington, nor paid advertising, nor "special events," which would cost in the neighborhood of $25,000 more, nor setting up a new website for the Turkmen embassy in Washington, which Schumacher hinted was essential and would cost the Maldon Group another "$35,000 and up."

This latter expense, admittedly, would be money well spent. I'd checked out the embassy's website while preparing for the project, and it looked like a parody site put together by *The*

Onion. The "Latest News" on the website dated back to September 18, 2000, and included a report of a scintillating phone conversation between the Turkmenbashi and the president of Uzbekistan. There was also a story titled "On virgin lands cotton is harvested with machines," and under a section headed "Business & Economy," readers learned that foreign investors were involved in 642 registered enterprises as of June 1, 1997.

I did a rough calculation in my head: in total, getting out our message about a new and improved Turkmenistan would require about $600,000 over the first year. I tried to radiate an air of sanguinity, to convey, I hoped, that for a firm such as the Maldon Group this was chump change. I made a vague gesture in the air with my hand that was meant to suggest my impatience with the trifling matter of money; what interested me now was the matter of what the Maldon Group would get for its payments.

APCO's strategy was laid out in a slide entitled "Elements of a Communications Program," of which there were four: "policy maker outreach," "media campaign," "coalition support," and "events." Thanks to its political contacts, APCO would have no problem in accomplishing the first component. In targeting Congress, it would pitch Turkmenistan hard to lawmakers who sat on "committees of jurisdiction," specifically Senators John Kerry and Norm Coleman at the Senate Foreign Relations Committee, and Congressmen Gary Ackerman and Mike Pence at the House Committee on Foreign Affairs.

APCO would also "identify members with interests in Turkmenistan," noting here Senator Sam Brownback, who has aggressively promoted American engagement with Caspian countries. More broadly, the firm would look to members of Congress who placed a high priority on "energy interests" and national security, as well as those who might have "home state linkages" with Turkmenistan. The slide cited Nevada as the sole example, because the state National Guard has had a program of cooperation with the Turkmen military since 1993. This supposedly would make members of the Nevada congressional delegation open to the idea of heightened engagement with the Berdymukhamedov regime, though it didn't sound like a particularly powerful selling point.

"Anyone who tells you they can get a congressman to do what you want ought not to be believed, but we can get in the door and make the case," Schumacher said. And when it got in the door, APCO would be armed with persuasive "fact sheets and other backgrounders" on key U.S.-Turkmenistan issues prepared by its in-house experts and PR specialists.

Meanwhile, APCO would coordinate its efforts with the Bush administration, especially at the State Department. It would also work closely, Schumacher promised, with the American embassy in Ashgabat. The Maldon Group's secret weapon here would be Elizabeth Jones, who noted that she had enjoyed a very close relationship with the current U.S. ambassador in Turkmenistan when she was in government and her relationship with him remained close.

As part of the outreach program to policymakers, APCO would arrange, without the slightest difficulty, meetings between key members of Congress and Turkmen officials it would bring to Washington. Would it be useful to have someone from the Maldon Group accompany visiting Turkmen officials around Capitol Hill? I asked. "It would be a minus, it might raise questions," Schumacher said. "But in certain circles—meetings with the energy [industry] or business-to-business meetings—your presence might be valuable."

APCO also would seek to organize a fact-finding trip to Turkmenistan by members of Congress or staffers. Given the scandal surrounding the lobbyist Jack Abramoff, it would be difficult and even unwise for the Maldon Group to sponsor a congressional trip directly, Schumacher said, but there would surely be official delegations traveling to the region, and "we have the contacts to urge them to stop there. It's more perception than reality. You can do it, but you have to be smart about it."

Robert Downen stepped in here, suggesting it was premature to rule out the possibility of organizing a private junket to Turkmenistan for a crew from Congress. True, the Maldon Group shouldn't organize it directly, but he'd had personal experience with academic groups sponsoring trips. "Maybe Turkmenistan has a think tank or university," he offered. "Under the old rules, any bona fide academic institution could sponsor [travel]. Under the new rules I'm not sure, but I can check."

As I later discovered, such a trip would still be legal under the new rules passed by Congress. These rules say that lobbying firms cannot pay for or arrange for congressional travel—with three exceptions: one-day trips, travel paid for by nonprofit groups, and travel paid for by universities. So the Maldon Group's very own congressional delegation to Turkmenistan would essentially be ready for boarding as soon as APCO found a Turkmen university willing to sponsor it.

Before discussion of the second part of APCO's communication program—the "media campaign"—Schumacher presented an overview of the current coverage. The bad news: almost all mentions of Turkmenistan were negative. On the upside, there wasn't very much coverage to speak of. Now was the time to strike.

Schumacher said two things were needed to "sell" Turkmenistan: a skillful firm, such as APCO, and a "good story," be it Turkmenistan's role as an energy supplier or the government increasing student exchanges or broadening Internet access.

Wasn't he worried, I asked, that the Turkmen regime would be held to impossibly high human rights standards? Schumacher sought to put my mind at ease. With any PR campaign there were bound to be "isolated incidents that look bad, and it's up to the communications company to figure out a way to be honest about them, to react and to put them in proper perspective, to make sure they don't derail the campaign." On the other hand, he allowed that something "really terrible"—the words dangled in the air—would be hard to overcome.

In fact, I later read in the corporate brochure that Schumacher had handed out earlier that APCO claimed special expertise in "Communicating in Times of Crisis" and "Managing the Aftermath." In the event of a public relations meltdown, clients could contact a special team—called the Crisis360 group—at any time of day or night. The brochure focused on corporate PR crises, but the strategies and tactics would certainly apply to foreign clients as well. "In today's 24-hour, global news cycle, the wrong actions may take just seconds, but the effects can last for years," the brochure warned. "Stories can move from the U.S. to Europe to Asia and back again, gathering momentum along the way."

APCO believed in preparing for the worst, so its Crisis360 group coached spokespersons for clients "to face the media and public in crisis situations" and run clients through "mock disaster response scenarios and realistic studio interview scenarios." The lobby shop's team would also be involved in "developing and testing crisis messages," with backing from another in-house unit called APCO Insight, which helps "clients convey the right message to the right people." And if something "really terrible" did happen—say, in the case of Turkmenistan, a famine or a political crackdown—APCO would be there for "post-crisis repositioning" as well. The Crisis360 group would not only help "avoid the perils of the unexpected," but also "seize the accompanying opportunity and leverage your challenge into forward momentum" with an aggressive "post-crisis strategy to reshape your public image."

So what might look to the untrained eye to be a brutal government crackdown could be better understood, with help from APCO's PR strategists, as merely a "disturbance," while protesters and reformers could be seen instead as menacing "rabble-rousers."

There was also the nagging question of public disclosure. Wasn't there a chance that by hiring a lobbying firm the Maldon Group would end up in the spotlight and lose our cherished anonymity, which was so vital to the success of our business model? Yes, Schumacher said, APCO would have to register and the Maldon Group would need to provide some additional information at that time, but there was no need to lose sleep over that. "We live up to the spirit and letter of the law, but we would provide minimal information," he said. "[We'd] say we're working for the Maldon Group on behalf of the government and would file semiannual reports. And that's it."

But what if we get calls from journalists? I asked.

"If they call you," Jones said with a big smile, "refer them to us."

A slide entitled "Core Media Relations Activities" flashed on the wall screen. It promised that APCO could "create news items and news outflow," organize media events, and identify and work with "key reporters." As this was her field of expertise, Dyck presented this slide. The media would be receptive to stories about Turkmenistan with the change of government, she said, plus "energy security is an additional hook. We can also bring things like Internet cafés to their attention." She said APCO shouldn't try to arrange a junket for journalists to travel to Turkmenistan, though it was possible that the firm might be able to find a foundation or other cutout to sponsor a media trip there. "You can't interfere with their [journalists'] work or it will backfire, but there are ways to get your message to the media," Schumacher added.

In addition to influencing news reports, Downen added, the firm could drum up positive op-eds in newspapers. "We can utilize some of the think-tank experts who would say, 'On the one hand this and the other hand that,' and we place it as a guest editorial." Schumacher said that APCO had someone on staff that "does nothing but that" and had succeeded in placing thousands of opinion pieces. Indeed, the slide that discussed this topic revealed that APCO didn't just recruit op-ed writers; the lobbying firm actually wrote the pieces and then went out and found "signatories" for its in-house work.

Schumacher warned me—apparently to demonstrate how ethical APCO was by comparison—that some lobbying firms would recommend that the Maldon Group pay for a four-page advertising insert for Turkmenistan in a major newspaper. That would be a big waste of money. "Those inserts are a joke," he said, and his colleagues around the table smiled knowingly. "Everyone laughs at them. They're only good for the *Post* and the *Washington Times*."

Discussion of the strategy's third item—building "coalition support," which meant developing seemingly independent and therefore more credible allies to offer favorable views of Turkmenistan—was brief. As a slide on the topic put it, we would need to start small, given that the "closed nature of country has inhibited investment and exchanges." For now, APCO would look for coalition partners within the energy and construction industries, which in the event of a thaw in relations would be the most likely future corporate investors in Turkmenistan. The firm would also put out feelers to "think tank experts and academics."

How precisely might we use think tanks and academics? I wondered aloud.

"I'm glad you asked," Schumacher said with a chuckle. He flipped to the next slide, which discussed the fourth element of the campaign: "Events." One possibility, Downen said, would be to hold a forum on U.S.-Turkmen relations, preferably built around a visit to the United States by a Turkmen official, hopefully the foreign minister or Berdymukhamedov himself. The more important the visiting VIP, said a slide that flashed on screen, the greater the opportunity for "high level press coverage and congressional outreach."

Possible hosts for a visiting Turkmen would include the Heritage Foundation, the Center for Strategic and International Studies, or the Council on Foreign Relations. "Last week I contacted a number of colleagues at think tanks," Downen went on. "Some real experts could easily be engaged to sponsor or host a public forum or panel that would bring in congressional staff and journalists."

The only cost would be refreshments and room rental— Schumacher joked that APCO would bake the cookies to save the Maldon Group a little money—and such an event could yield a tremendous payoff. "If we can get a paper published or a speech at a conference, we can get a friendly member of Congress to insert that in the *Congressional Record* and get that printed and send it out," Schumacher said. "So you take one event and get it multiplied."

Such an event would "play well into dealing with the media," Dyck agreed. "Think tank people get quoted in the press. If we can get them receptive to changes, they could end up doing a lot of good."

Another option, Schumacher explained, would be to pay *Roll Call* and *The Economist* to host a Turkmenistan event. It would be costlier than the think-tank route, perhaps around $25,000, but in compensation we would have tighter control over the proceedings, plus gain "the imprimatur of a respected third party." In order that the event not seem like paid advertising, the title for the event should be "bigger than your theme," Schumacher explained, even as it would be put together in a way "that you get your message across."

So we wouldn't call it "Turkmenistan Day"? I asked.

No, Schumacher replied. "Energy Security" would be a better theme.

"Or 'Caspian Basin Pipelines,' " Jones added.

"That's how you do it," Schumacher said. The Maldon Group wouldn't have its own speaker on the dais, but APCO would line up a few people—possibilities included an administration official or an executive from an American firm involved in Turkmenistan—to speak for us. While promising reform was important, we would probably want to focus on matters like energy and regional security. "In a world where the administration wants some realism, there may be ways to get positive messages out," Schumacher said.

If we hired APCO, the firm would commence with a thirty-day blitzkrieg, the lobbying equivalent of a military "shock and awe" campaign. The firm's troops would fan out across Washington to consult with policymakers and obtain a "baseline" view of where Turkmenistan stood in official circles and gain an understanding of the Berdymukhamedov regime's PR strengths and weaknesses. APCO would also put in place a "media monitoring system," which to my ear sounded like a fancy means (and no doubt a pricey one for the Maldon Group) of using Google and media databases to keep track of what was being written about Turkmenistan. Based on this intelligence gathering, APCO would, during the opening thirty-day onslaught, prepare "position papers" on key topics, hold first meetings with policymakers, make probes on Turkmenistan's behalf with embassy officials in Ashgabat, and prepare an initial Washington event at which, like an Auto Show featuring this year's models, the new and improved Turkmen regime would be rolled out.

As the PowerPoint presentation neared the close, a new slide laid out the broad benefits that the Maldon Group could expect to see in exchange for the large checks we'd be writing to APCO. These included raising "decision-maker awareness" of Turkmenistan, especially its profile and visibility "as a nation important to the United States," and building a "broader base of support" for the country. APCO would also improve media portrayals of Turkmenistan. It conceded that it would be impossible to "end negative coverage"—a tacit admission that the facts on the ground under Berdymukhamedov were unlikely to change dramatically for the better—but it would find a way to "get positive messages out."

A final sales point made during the presentation was that APCO had core principles. The Maldon Group should consider this when making its decision about which firm to hire. APCO viewed "client relationships as long-term strategic partnerships," said a concluding slide, and measured itself "by what we achieve for our clients." Sure, the achievements in this case would redound to the benefit of a sleazy energy firm and a Stalinist dictatorship, and yes, APCO would be a willing shill for one of the world's worst regimes without performing the simplest due diligence. But APCO cared deeply about clients like the Maldon Group and wouldn't be satisfied until it had fulfilled its promises to us.

In an era of poor customer service and shoddy workmanship, APCO's devotion to clients was indeed heartening. Under different circumstances—had I been posing, for example, as the head of a pro-democracy group looking for U.S. backing or the director of a Turkmen orphanage seeking American funding—I might have gotten choked up.

The meeting with APCO had been going on for more than an hour, and up until this point, no one had asked Ricardo or me a single question about the Maldon Group or our personal backgrounds. Finally, Schumacher very carefully raised an obvious question: How exactly was it that I had gotten involved in the Maldon Group and the Turkmen gas business?

This was the cue to launch into the story I'd constructed to explain the odd set of circumstances that had led to my position with the Maldon Group. I began with my formative years in St. Louis, mentioning here that I'd grown up a fanatical fan of Cardinal baseball, and my powerful memories of listening to the famous broadcaster Harry Caray announce the games on KMOX Radio, which was broadcast across the Midwest. There were knowing smiles around the table—clearly the Redbirds had loyal fans at APCO.

Then I quickly rolled through my university years, the detour to Brazil, the Lebanese girlfriend I'd met there, and my subsequent hiring by her father. "But don't you have any business or financial background?" Schumacher wanted to know. He seemed satisfied with my explanation of how I just made the trains run on time, and how neither Ricardo nor I had ever been to Turkmenistan.

I braced for probing follow-up questions, but there were none forthcoming other than a peculiar and unexpected query from Elizabeth Jones. Was it possible, she asked with a big smile on her face, that she knew my boss? She'd met a London-based Middle Eastern trader with Caspian interests during her years in the government, and she had a hunch that he was my present employer.

I had no idea who she was thinking of, but this was not a welcome subject, particularly as there was no good answer to the question since I had no boss in London. I didn't want to look as if I was stonewalling, but also didn't want to heighten Jones's curiosity, which might prompt her to look into the matter further. That could only lead to trouble. "It's possible you would have met him," I said mysteriously, trusting that she wouldn't press the issue.

She didn't, and the meeting was over. After a series of firm handshakes, I promised I would be back in touch as soon as I had consulted with my superiors in London.

EARLY THE FOLLOWING MORNING I RECEIVED AN E-MAIL FROM SCHU-macher. "On behalf of all my colleagues, I want to thank you for meeting with us yesterday," he wrote. "I hope you took away from our meeting a good sense of our capabilities, experience and expertise. I also hope you took away from it a good sense of who we are and how we think about projects like the one you are suggesting." He and his colleagues "enjoyed the discussion thoroughly," he said, and told me to make sure to let him know if I needed any more information before discussing my round of meetings in Washington with Maldon Group officials in London.

"We enjoyed the meeting and were impressed with your team," I replied. "We'll be back in touch soon."

Then I dashed out the door to meet Ricardo and head over to a morning meeting with Cassidy & Associates.

SIX

Cassidy & Associates:
The Belly of the Beast

APCO WORLDWIDE IS A TOP NAME IN WASHINGTON INFLUENCE peddling, but Cassidy & Associates, where I had a meeting scheduled at 9:30 A.M. on February 28, is perhaps the lobbying world's biggest name. In the midst of my Turkmeniscam sting, *The Washington Post* ran a sprawling and ultimately flattering twenty-seven-part newspaper and online series chronicling Cassidy's rise to the top of the Beltway heap. The series, which debuted just four days after my meeting with the firm, called Gerald Cassidy "a godfather of the influence business" and the proprietor of "the most lucrative lobbying firm" in town. His company had succeeded at helping clients such as Ocean Spray get its fruit juices into public school systems and defense giant General Dynamics preserve the Seawolf submarine project (a $1 billion boondoggle for taxpayers), and had won hundreds of millions of dollars' worth of earmarks for a variety of customers. "For years . . . Cassidy and his colleagues could truthfully tell prospective clients that they never failed to win an earmark for an institution that had retained them," the story said.

At the heart of the firm's success, said the *Post*, was a less than startling revelation that Cassidy had made years earlier: "members of Congress who helped his clients could be thanked with campaign contributions." Armed with this insight, he, his wife, and Cassidy's employees and their spouses had made at least $5.3 million in combined political donations to the two major political parties and their candidates. "The lobbyists of Cassidy & Associates had received many times that much in fees from their clients," the *Post* reported. "The clients had received hundreds of millions in earmarked appropriations and other benefits worth hundreds of millions more."

I had the APCO meeting under my belt, which was a big relief. But given Cassidy's grand reputation, I was even more nervous on Day 2 as Ricardo I sat in the backseat of a taxi en route to the firm's headquarters. Cassidy is located just a block away from APCO, but the setting was more elegant, and more intimidating. The firm occupies the entire fourth floor of its building, so that one enters the offices upon exiting the elevator. When Ricardo and I walked in and announced ourselves, a receptionist coolly instructed us to have a seat in a waiting area to her left.

A few minutes later, she escorted us into a large conference room with a beautiful wood table polished to a bright sheen. There were about twenty seats around the table, and eight places had been laid out with a glass, each set atop a paper coaster embossed with the firm's name. The table also held an assortment of canned soft drinks, a pitcher of ice water with lemon slices, a cup of sharpened pencils, and a pile of yellow legal pads.

A phalanx of six Cassidy officials soon entered the conference room in formation, all dressed in elegant business attire of varying shades of black, gray, and navy blue. There was Chuck Dolan, whom I'd spoken to during the conference call; Gordon Speed, the firm's pudgy, baby-faced director of business development; tall, thin Gerald Warburg, a former Hill staffer and company vice president; Christy Moran, who during the meeting told me she had previously worked for Saudi Arabia and helped boost its image with an "allies program" that sent visitors to the country; and David Bartlett, another PR specialist whose firm biography said he had helped corporate CEOs "face the nation's toughest journalists."

The sixth member of the Cassidy team, and its clear leader, was firm vice chairman Gregg Hartley, who with his crew cut and serious manner initially reminded me of a drill sergeant; but soon he loosened up and proved to possess a certain folksy appeal. After the introductions, Hartley passed Ricardo and me a few handouts, including a colorful corporate brochure, featuring on its cover a nighttime photograph of a glowing Capitol dome.

I flipped through the pages with interest, as I kept an eye on Hartley. Cassidy, said the brochure, offered "A Tradition of Ethics and Integrity that goes to the core of our beliefs." It also made the claim—a brazenly cynical one even by the standards of Washington—that Gerald Cassidy had founded the firm "to ensure that Americans have access and the ability to exercise their First Amendment right to petition their government." Well, Americans (and foreigners) able to pay Cassidy's fat rates, anyway.

The brochure said there was only "one certainty in Washington—change." Policymakers were constantly tinkering with laws, policies, and regulations, and the decisions they made had far-reaching impacts in the United States and around the world. "One vote in Congress or one agency's regulatory action can truly transform an industry," the brochure said. "In response, today's organizations must anticipate, understand and adapt to the ever changing government landscape." Fortunately, Cassidy was there to help.

As I glanced through the brochure, Hartley offered an overview of Cassidy's general operations and client base. He said one other thing, though, that concerned me: after he and his colleagues made their presentation, they'd like me to tell them more about the Maldon Group. He didn't say it in an unfriendly or suspicious way, but neither were there understanding words about knowing that I would probably need to be brief given my previously stated demand for confidentiality.

At least, I thought, I'd only have to give my spiel about the Maldon Group after I had heard Cassidy's entire pitch. Even if I muffed it badly, I'd almost surely get out the door; Cassidy might discover through belated due diligence that there was something seriously amiss with my story, but at least I wouldn't be busted on the premises. Still, the knowledge that Hartley and his colleagues were expecting to hear more about the Maldon Group later hung over me throughout the meeting.

During our conference call, Hartley had hammered on the theme of Cassidy's powerful Beltway connections, and he returned to that subject now. His firm, he said, had "strong personal relationships" with policymakers, and not just to a committee chairman here and there, as was the case with some of its competitors. Cassidy had ties across the board—at the staff level and the committee level, with the Republican and Democratic leadership and the administration. Among the handouts Hartley had passed out was a copy of a *Congressional Quarterly* article that identified key members of new House majority leader Nancy Pelosi's "Inner Circle." Among those prominently featured was Cassidy CEO Martin Russo, a former Democratic congressman whom the article described as Pelosi's "family friend" who was "helping her rebuild ties to K Street" after her party's capture of Congress in the 2006 elections.

Hartley pointedly noted that he knew the Maldon Group was meeting with other firms, but said we'd "have a hard time matching [the] types of successes" Cassidy had racked up. Hartley pointed to his firm's work on behalf of Equatorial Guinea, a pariah state like Turkmenistan. But thanks to Cassidy, things were now looking up for the government there. The proof, as he'd mentioned during the conference call as well, was that just three years earlier, *Parade* magazine had ranked Obiang as "the world's sixth worst dictator." He grimaced as he uttered that last word, but at least he managed to spit it out this time. "He's still not a great guy," Hartley went on as a few of his colleagues suppressed grins, "but he's not in the top ten anymore, and we can take some credit for helping them figure out how to work down that list. Is he going to win the UN humanitarian award next year? No, he's not, but we're making progress."

Cassidy's strategic communications team, working "on an offensive and defensive basis," now ran all media relations for Equatorial Guinea. "We've taken them to a whole new level," Hartley said.

Here he offered more proof of Cassidy's success for Obiang—which, he later let slip, as a means of priming me for a talk about money, was costing his government $2.4 million per year: until quite recently, the United States had no embassy in Equatorial Guinea. About eighteen months earlier, he related, his firm had taken a group of Hill staffers to that country. "There's a reputation that staffers like to go to cushy places where you have a couple of meetings and go to the beach and play golf, but Equatorial Guinea is not like that," he continued. "It's hard to convince people to spend more than twelve daylight hours there. But we took a group there and they were impressed enough with the changes and especially with U.S. interests in the region and in that country"—he was referring to oil—"and that we were not protecting those interests well enough. In a matter of months we got the embassy reopened there. That's a huge success for Equatorial Guinea."

This surely was an impressive achievement. It was also a huge pile of bullshit that bore no relationship to how the United States had in fact come to reopen its embassy in Equatorial Guinea. Kenneth Case of the Maldon Group could easily have found out the true story after the meeting with a few minutes' worth of research. Having written about it extensively, I knew immediately that Hartley's story was as bogus as my own tale about the Maldon Group's stake in Turkmenistan.

What actually had happened was that in 1994, the American ambassador in Malabo, John Bennett, was threatened with death after calling for improved human rights conditions. The threat came in a message thrown from the window of a passing vehicle—which eyewitnesses said was driven by a government official—that warned Bennett, "You will go to America as a corpse." Several years later, the Clinton administration shut down the U.S. embassy in Malabo, and relations were subsequently handled from Cameroon.

But as Equatorial Guinea's oil reserves grew, and American corporate interest deepened, a slow thaw emerged in bilateral relations. In June 2000, the Overseas Private Investment Corporation approved up to $373 million in loan guarantees and political-risk insurance for construction of a methanol plant in Equatorial Guinea, its largest program ever in sub-Saharan Africa.

The thaw quickened after Bush took office, in response to intense lobbying from the oil industry. "It is important to underscore that most of the oil and gas concessions awarded in Equatorial Guinea to date have been awarded to US firms," read a memo drafted on behalf of the oil companies and sent to Bush in mid-2001. "This is in stark contrast to neighboring countries in the region, where the United States has consistently lost out to French and other European and Asian competitors." Several months later, in November of that year, the administration quietly authorized the reopening of a new U.S. embassy in Malabo. This was three years before Cassidy had even registered to represent the country.

No matter. Ricardo and I exchanged a look to show that we were favorably impressed. With Cassidy on board, President Berdymukhamedov's enhanced standing with American policymakers and the public was all but assured.

Now Warburg took over the meeting, assuring us that there was "tremendous interest" at the highest level of the U.S. government in the relationship with Turkmenistan—far more, he said, than what might be believed based on a perusal of *Parade* magazine, which perennially had listed Niyazov, along with Obiang, as one of the world's worst dictators. What was needed was to take the government's newfound interest in Turkmenistan and "make that manifest" in the media. "We need a new story to attract people," he said confidently. "You need a new angle, whether it's the Iran angle or the energy angle or the drug interdiction angle. There are a lot of stories that aren't public—the only one that is public is the dictator story, the cult of personality."

"A lot depends on what happens next, but you have a hook here with the new government and how it's different from the old government," Dolan said. "That's something that journalists and think tanks are going to be interested in."

Warburg talked with some passion about two "remarkable

lobbying campaigns" that the firm had been involved with, both of which had succeeded in getting the U.S. government to move "against its express will." The first was eliminating a longtime trade embargo against Vietnam, which the firm had achieved over the opposition of the families of POWs and MIAs. The key to success was assembling an outside pressure group called the Multinational Business Development Coalition, which was made up of major American corporations seeking business in Vietnam. "The U.S. had no relations," Warburg said. "We changed that policy, ended the embargo, and opened Vietnam up to U.S. economic exchange."

The second campaign, Warburg said, involved winning permission in 1995 for President Lee Teng-hui of Taiwan to make a private visit to the United States "over the express opposition of the executive branch." At the time, Taiwan's embassy wasn't even allowed to lobby in Washington without permission from the State Department. Evading that obstacle was simple: since the government couldn't retain Cassidy, a Taiwanese think tank fronting for it did. President Bill Clinton had said he wouldn't allow Lee to come to the United States, so Cassidy, Warburg recounted, began a campaign to lobby Congress. After both chambers passed resolutions in support of a visit by Lee, the White House caved. "The president of the United States reversed policy," said Warburg. The campaign had been so brilliant, in fact, that graduate students had written theses on it.

Warburg also mentioned his past work for Merhav, the large Israeli firm with major interests in Turkmenistan for which Cassidy had obtained Export-Import Bank financing for a trans-Caspian pipeline. Unlike the case with other lobbying firms the Maldon Group might hire, "we really know Turkmenistan. It wouldn't be on-the-job training for us."

In fact, "one of the first benchmarks" in the Merhav contract was to arrange for Niyazov to visit Washington. "We succeeded against great odds," Warburg said. "A state visit wasn't in the cards, but it wasn't just think tanks and the State Department either"—Niyazov had met in 1998 with then vice president Al Gore. Niyazov wasn't as notorious back then as he became during his later years, but the Washington visit by the Turkmenbashi had been a legitimate lobbying coup by Cassidy. Warburg said that Cassidy's representation of Merhav had been "facilitated by our friends in the executive branch," and he'd expect similar assistance if the Maldon Group retained his firm now.

Once more I tried to look suitably impressed. It sure was encouraging, I said, that Cassidy had been able to achieve such victories during the Niyazov days. That certainly augured well for my firm now.

When Warburg had represented Merhav, he continued, he'd met a number of Turkmen officials. Unfortunately, those old contacts might no longer be useful because "the previous government had a history of shuffling ministers," he said. "I won't pursue the metaphor."

To which Hartley added, "We won't ask where all of them were shuffled!" There was general merriment, which seemed bizarrely inappropriate given the ghastly realities of Turkmenistan. In 2006, sixteen ministers had been jailed or sent into internal exile, and one of them was believed to have died in prison.

Cassidy saw its strategy as having two central prongs, one targeting policymakers and the other targeting the media. Bringing Turkmen officials to Washington was also a must, though we needed to be realistic. If the Maldon Group said it wanted Berdymukhamedov to address a joint session of Congress, Cassidy would tell you that's not possible, Warburg said. On the other hand, might Cassidy be able to arrange "a coffee in the Senate

Foreign Relations hearing room of the U.S. Capitol where the foreign minister is warmly received?" Yes, it very well might.

A few days earlier, I'd e-mailed Gordon Speed a list of questions I wanted to have addressed during the meeting. Hartley noted the list and congratulated me for putting together such "astute" queries. Among the questions I'd asked had been whether it would be advisable to arrange a trip to Turkmenistan for members of Congress. Hartley said that it was, but it would be critical to pick "the right members of Congress," which he defined as those with "a leaning that will be instrumental in us making progress on our representation." As at APCO, the Cassidy team said that the post-Abramoff climate would make it harder to arrange a private trip for members of Congress—"but not impossible," in Hartley's words. In the meantime, a less visible trip for Hill staffers could be more easily accomplished.

Dolan spoke up, saying that the Maldon Group should not underestimate the value of arranging a trip to Turkmenistan for journalists and think tank analysts, which was something he had done on behalf of an organization called the Valdai International Discussion Club. During the meeting, Dolan simply described the program as a way to give people "firsthand information" about Russia and mentioned that past participants had included Ariel Cohen of the Heritage Foundation, Marshall Goldman of Harvard, and Jim Hoagland of *The Washington Post*. A similar program might work for Turkmenistan, he suggested.

Later, I discovered that a program modeled on the Valdai International Discussion Club would indeed have been helpful to the Maldon Group's cause. The club was set up in September 2004 by pro-government outfits like the Russian News and Information Agency and the Council for Foreign and Defense Policy. It offered all-expense-paid trips to Russia for selected Westerners. Amid the general pampering, the visiting academics and reporters were granted audiences with senior Russian political figures.

After returning from his Valdai-paid trip in 2006, Hoagland wrote a critical but not entirely unflattering story about Vladimir Putin, whom he and other junketeers had met "at his sprawling dacha in suburban Moscow." The Russian president had taken questions from the group "between servings of octopus carpaccio, baked sea bass and figs with yogurt sorbet, all prepared by his Italian chef and washed down by an unassuming Pinot Grigio."

Other Valdai Club members were even more helpful. "Permanent Normal Trade Relations for Russia Would Benefit the U.S. and Russia" was the title of a report Cohen co-authored for the Heritage Foundation after his junket. "The growing Russian market is an opportunity that American businesses cannot and should not miss," the report said.

Junketeer Stefan Wagstyl took a similar position in an article in the *Financial Times*. If the Bush administration failed to deepen economic ties with Russia, it risked "undermining" Putin and "playing into the hands of the *siloviki*—conservative hardliners linked to the security services." The article quoted an unnamed official as saying, "If this decision is not taken now, don't be surprised if the *siloviki* win in Russia." Wagstyl did note the obvious, namely that Putin was a former KGB officer who had "often sided with the *siloviki* in his drive to consolidate the Kremlin's authority." But the unnamed official said Putin had "also retained liberal advisers" and that for "young reformers," among whom he included himself, "Putin is our hope."

Hartley said that at the present time, all the attention on Turkmenistan was negative. That had to stop. "There's a need to identify journalists and policymakers with self-serving reasons" to give the Berdymukhamedov regime a fair shake, he said. Cassidy would find open-minded people—maybe they were interested in securing energy resources, or maybe they were focused on national security—"and get them to believe that now is the time for them to play a role. We have to make them care, and care at this time."

For his part, Warburg said that "the more folks we can get to go in" the better, especially if Cassidy could arrange for them to "give an exit interview at the airport saying things are looking up, improving, changing." Of course, that might not be the case, but who cared as long as someone who appeared to be independent was saying so to reporters. Perception was everything.

I agreed enthusiastically with the strategy being laid out by Cassidy's lobbyists. It was all about finding the right talking points. "One of the best hooks we have is energy security," I said, employing lingo I'd heard the day before at APCO. "That's an obvious story we want to tell."

"There's a need for sophistication [when] talking to very experienced reporters who are experts," Dolan stated, and he was clearly suggesting that the Maldon Group needed Cassidy to serve as an intermediary with the media. "They can tell if you have the knowledge or not."

"I'd add that it's invaluable to have third-party supporters who can be used to boost the image of the country—think tank analysts, members of the academic community, energy security experts," Christy Moran added in another barely disguised sales pitch. "We're hired by a lot of clients who don't want attention [on] themselves, they want it on the issues."

Now came the moment I had been dreading. Hartley announced that he and his colleagues had a few questions about the Maldon Group.

I would be as helpful as possible, I replied, but I had to preface this part of the conversation by reemphasizing that there wasn't a lot I could share at this point of preliminary conversations. While it pained me "to look like I'm being evasive," discretion was our firm's very lifeblood, and I was hamstrung until—if we picked Cassidy—we signed a confidentiality agreement.

"We're going to ask questions, and you may have to throw the wall up," Hartley said reassuringly. "Don't mention names if you can't mention names."

The questions were quite easy to handle. I did little more than toss out the same scraps of information I had given earlier to Cassidy and the other firms. We were a small group of British, Middle Eastern, and Eastern European investors. We had a close relationship with the government, but there were no Turkmen officials involved in the Maldon Group. We knew a few people at the Turkmen equivalent of the National Security Council, but I was not authorized to say whom. It was unfortunate, I added, that a colleague from the Maldon Group's Moscow office had been unable to come to Washington for the meetings, but she could not get away. The requirements of discretion would have limited the information she could have provided, but she was better informed about Turkmenistan, and the natural gas trade, than either Ricardo or I and might have been able to shed some additional light.

And that was it. The Cassidy team was placated.

Ricardo had sat silently throughout the meeting, and we'd agreed going in that he should say at least a few words. I was running out of steam, so I turned to him and asked him to talk about his role at the Maldon Group.

"I have the awful task to conduit—I mean to conduct—meetings with potential people who are interested, and being capital providers for the project," he began in a rambling statement that sounded like something out of Lewis Carroll's "Jabberwocky." "Usually like Ken was talking about it, okay, there's personal return that bring benefits, et cetera, et cetera, et cetera. In other words, to diversify investments—how you bring those diversified investments into a direct foreign investment in this kind of political atmosphere such as this country."

As Ricardo rambled on, members of the Cassidy team were looking increasingly baffled. I was starting to get panicky, but merely nodded my head to suggest that I found his incomprehensible chatter perfectly lucid. "Some people don't want to, again, reveal who they are, et cetera, et cetera, et cetera," he continued. "But the . . . structuring investments in itself can be very creative, you know, it depends which banks are involved in bringing the money, et cetera, who represents the clients and again it's what kind of profits they're going to get out of this, that's the bottom line—like Ken mentioned, the interest in this, they want to see the final product . . ."

I finally jumped in with what even under the circumstances amounted to a non sequitur. "At this point, though, our interest is strictly financial." The meeting lurched along, and I soon added, "Our incentive, bluntly, is to strengthen our position over there."

"We assumed that," Warburg said with a big smile, and the room cracked up.

Meanwhile, Hartley interjected, saying to my amazement that he knew just what Ricardo had been talking about because Gerald Cassidy, the head of the firm, ran a merchant banking operation that was not connected to the lobby shop but that did "similar things." Similar to what, I wanted to ask, but it seemed wise to move on.

In fact, I had a few questions of my own. How rigorous were the public disclosure requirements for this kind of lobbying program? I asked. Would journalists be calling us up and asking questions?

Hartley said Cassidy would have legal counsel review the matter, but based on what he had heard so far, part of the Maldon Group's program was "not necessarily reportable at all," though any direct lobbying of members of Congress or administration officials would need to be disclosed. But he assured me I could rest easy. "We have to disclose who we represent, but there doesn't have to be great detail," he said. "There's absolutely no reason at all that this ought to focus on you. The way we would handle this, there'd be very little about you and virtually none about your investors."

Warburg could understand why "your investors would be anxious about that," but agreed there was no cause for alarm. During the eight years that Cassidy had represented Merhav, the Israeli firm's "name never appeared in an American newspaper. . . . They did get press in Ashgabat, they had a picture with the president, [but that] was helpful."

Hartley said he wanted to reply to one of the questions I had previously e-mailed: "Won't any message we seek to convey be discounted or simply dismissed as overly favorable to the government's position?"

Given how cynical people were nowadays, that was a legitimate concern. "Everyone wants to discount your message, and they have a million reasons to do that," he said in a tone of regret. "This is where you bring intelligence to the table. The relationship you have on the ground [in Turkmenistan], coupled with what we have done on behalf of similar clients, helps us figure out how to begin chipping away at the animosity and the negativity and inaccurate perceptions—and when they're accurate, just start chipping away with whatever gains we can get to turn that around."

For at least the third time during the meeting, a member of Cassidy's team—Hartley in this case—used the term "incremental" to describe the type of PR gains we could expect to achieve on behalf of Turkmenistan. "You need a long-term engagement to be successful," he said. The emphasis was on the word "long."

This led inexorably to the question of money, specifically how much of it the Maldon Group would need to hire Cassidy. As it turned out, APCO, at least in comparison, had been cheap. For Turkmenistan, Hartley said, there could be no quick, easy solutions; hence, he proposed a three-year effort at from $1.2 million to $1.5 million annually—and that could run higher, he warned, if a do-gooder organization such as a human rights group targeted the regime, necessitating intensified spin control by the firm's lobbyists. "Others will do it for less, but you won't get people with our experience, our knowledge of Turkmenistan, our ties to [the government]," Warburg said. "I can give you the numbers for some one-man shops that will underbid us by 10 percent—don't waste your time." Some PR firms would throw together a Turkmen caucus in Congress and "bamboozle three members into joining it and say, 'See, we succeeded.' Well, that's baloney, that's not what you need here."

"We may do a caucus, but . . ." Hartley said with a smile, and everyone in the room erupted in laughter. "You've looked at our bios," he said after things settled down. "Look at our track record and what we've charged for other representations . . . and you'll see you're not being gouged."

I didn't write the checks, I said, but the figure certainly seemed reasonable to me.

When it was time for the hard sell, Warburg gave me a piece of information he had picked up—something, he said, for me to share "with your friends and investors back in England." The previous week, he claimed, there had been a meeting on Turkmenistan at the highest level of the U.S. government. "We'd like to make sure you're on the agenda for the next such meeting," he said pointedly. "We'd like to be involved in prepping the individuals before such a meeting, and we'd like to be involved in interpreting the outcome to your investors, and through you to the government in a way that really empowers you in that market."

Hartley, too, emphasized how interested Cassidy was in winning the contract. "This is the sort of thing we do extremely well," he said at one point. "It's the kind of stuff that gets our juices flowing."

"You're definitely on the short list," I said.

"The good end of the list?" Warburg quipped, and the room again roared with laughter.

"The right end," I assured them all.

The meeting was coming to an end. "I admire the challenges you're facing," Warburg confided during the round of handshakes on the way out the door.

Only in Washington, I thought, would selling a Stalinist dictatorship amount to an estimable task.

SOON AFTER OUR MEETING IN WASHINGTON, GORDON SPEED E-MAILED me "in London" to propose a follow-up conference call with Hartley and to say that Cassidy wanted to "submit a more formal proposal detailing our plan for a possible future engagement with your company. Our hope is that this document would help give you a better understanding of our proposed strategy." Needless to say, I accepted this generous offer.

During the subsequent phone conversation, Hartley proposed that the Maldon Group and Cassidy sign a confidentiality agreement before the firm sent its proposal. I declined. Several other firms had made a similar request, I said, but our counsel had refused, as he didn't want to review and keep track of a bunch of meaningless agreements. We would only sign such an agreement with the firm that was picked to handle the Turkmenistan account.

Hartley understood. Cassidy would send its proposal, but it might have to be a bit more "generic" as a result.

In order to help prepare the proposal, Warburg asked a few questions, including one about the nature of our ties to the new "authorities" in Ashgabat. I decided I'd better think that over before replying, so I promised to get back to Cassidy after speaking with the Maldon Group's counsel for guidance. I e-mailed back in a few days to say that I could pass on only the following: "The Maldon Group has had a strong, positive relationship with the government, and that remains the case under the new president. As I mentioned at our meeting, we don't foresee any business problems arising with the change. We have good contacts at several key agencies, including (the rough equivalent of) the National Security Council."

Soon thereafter, Speed e-mailed me Cassidy's proposal. (He offered to mail me a hard copy, but since there was nowhere he could send it, I said that would not be necessary.) Signed by Hartley, the twelve-page document covered some of the same ground that we'd previously discussed, including the firm's stellar access to policymakers. "My connection to the House Republican Leadership is arguably unsurpassed by any other group or individual in Washington," Hartley wrote.

Hartley would lead Cassidy's Turkmen team, which, in addition to the officials I had met in Washington, would include a few other key people from the firm. There would be Kai Anderson, who had worked for nearly six years in the office of Senate majority leader Harry Reid, where he'd handled energy issues. We'd also count on help from some Cassidy staffers with GOP connections: Christy Evans, who had "steadfast ties to Republican leaders in Congress," and Christine O'Connor, who had previously worked for retired congressman William F. Goodling and had been "a Republican observer for the George W. Bush Florida Recount team in Palm Beach County" during the disputed 2000 presidential election. That seemed like just the sort of experience that would come in handy during an upcoming Turkmen election.

The proposal's "Plan of Action," which described how Cassidy would "undertake a targeted, integrated initiative . . . to improve Turkmenistan's reputation as a viable economic and diplomatic partner" of the United States, contained some interesting details as well. As described by the firm, its lobbyists would educate senior government officials and opinion makers "on positive developments taking place in Turkmenistan," and would sell the country on the basis of its "strategic importance in Central Asia" and the "critical role" it could play in American energy security. Furthermore, Cassidy promised to inform target audiences about "common interests" between Washington and Ashgabat, and in the case of government officials, "advise them on steps they can take to strengthen our bilateral ties."

Cassidy's preliminary research had already determined that there was "accelerated interest" in Turkmenistan at the highest levels of the U.S. government. This was a great opportunity, since it would make it easier to reach out to government officials as well as the media, but it also presented a challenge, as "greater attention can bring greater scrutiny."

Of course, "attention" and "scrutiny" are essentially synonymous; the only reason that more of it posed a challenge to Cassidy's proposed lobbying campaign was that in the case of Turkmenistan, the truth was almost never good. Cassidy had in fact already uncovered troubling news: "We have become aware," the proposal said ominously, "of U.S. determination to

aggressively push an agenda of human rights and democratic reforms in exchange for greater engagement with Ashgabat."

This supposed discovery was surely a scare tactic. The Bush
administration had openly prioritized trade and business promotion, not human rights, with other major Caspian energy producers. And a well-placed source told me at the time that State
Department officials had made it very clear that the Bush administration's major policy goal in Turkmenistan was seeking to
open the country to investment by U.S. energy firms.

To deal with the threat of scrutiny, Cassidy would seek to
drive "the story being told about Turkmenistan by the media,
rather than merely reacting to it. By engaging with correspondents, we will coordinate a global message about political, social
and economic progress."

Like APCO, the firm would recruit friendly authors—a "well-
respected scholar" or an official from an influential foreign company "with large-scale investments in the region"—for op-eds it
could plant in newspapers. Cassidy would also put together "a
list of potential vulnerabilities, such as humanitarian issues, social conditions and otherwise. . . . With these issues in mind, we
will conduct 'worst-case' scenario planning and response development by anticipating crises, preparing spokespeople, [and]
drafting statements." In other words, Cassidy would have an
emergency response network in place should, for example, opposition members happen to be mowed down by government
guns.

All of this would be done with input from the Turkmen embassy in Washington, "to ensure that our messages are coordinated and none of our activities are duplicated." And not only
would Cassidy doll up Turkmenistan's image, it would simultaneously "enhance" the Maldon Group's business objectives. "We
will be your eyes and ears in Washington, D.C.," the proposal

said. "We will recommend initiatives and execute them. We will help you be an even more effective, and attractive, strategic partner for your colleagues in Turkmenistan. They will come to rely on you ever more, valuing your insights and appreciating your initiatives."

MEANWHILE, APCO, TOO, WAS GROVELING TO WIN THE TURKMENISTAN deal. In March, Schumacher e-mailed to ask for "an update on where the Maldon Group is on potentially retaining a firm here in DC to assist the Turkmenistan government." I should let him know if there was "anything else you need from us" before making a decision. That same month, after being told that the Maldon Group had still not made a decision, Schumacher e-mailed again to say that he was soon coming to London on business: "If APCO is still under consideration to be your partner on the Turkmenistan initiative, and if there is any value, I would be delighted to meet with you and your colleagues on Thursday at a time and location of your choice," he wrote. "That way, if there is more you would like to know about us, or if you feel you wish us to be your partner, we could either answer questions or move the effort forward."

This threw me into a brief panic, as the Maldon Group, being nonexistent, had no London office, and I was of course in Washington, D.C., so I couldn't possibly meet with Schumacher. I e-mailed back to say that the Maldon Group would in fact be making its decision on which lobby firm to hire the very next day and that I'd let him know the outcome; whatever the decision, I would be traveling in the Middle East with my boss and unable to see him when he came to London.

Schumacher, hopeful that APCO was about to win the fat Turkmen contract, e-mailed right back: "Thanks. I look forward

to your update. I would be happy to meet with anyone you think I should. If after your meeting tomorrow you want me to get together with your colleagues, just give me their coordinates and I will be in touch with them to set up a time."

I was starting to feel guilty; I had to keep reminding myself that APCO's hope here was to make big bucks by sprinkling perfume on the rotten Berdymukhamedov regime and hoping no one whiffed the underlying stench. In any case, I couldn't keep delaying, so the next day I gave Schumacher the bad news: the Maldon Group had decided to hire a different Washington lobby shop. Schumacher took the news badly. "Needless to say, we are disappointed," he replied. "When we do not get work we always try to find out why and what, if anything, we could have done better. Feedback?"

I sent an e-mail back offering my condolences, and saying it had been "a very hard call." Schumacher wrote again to say, "If something changes, please feel free to contact us. We enjoyed our meeting with you and would welcome a future opportunity to assist you."

Cassidy & Associates was so arrogant, and was so sure that I would pick it for the job, that turning it down was more delicate. In late March, in reply to a few requests for a status report, I e-mailed Speed. "We met yesterday and I'm afraid I have a reply that you will find frustrating," I wrote. "We're still interested in pursuing the project, and your team would be a likely choice if we do so. But there is some doubt here about whether to move forward given the uncertainty of results and a few other questions."

I went on to explain that my boss "will be spending a lot of time in the Middle East over the next two months, and several other investors will be mostly away from London as well." As a result, the Maldon Group had decided to delay its decision, but

I'd be returning to Washington in mid-June and we might want to meet again with firm officials at that time.

Speed thanked me for my "thoughtful and candid response," and said he understood our dilemma. "This is a very important decision and should not be made without an honest and thorough assessment of your needs, objectives, and our likelihood of achieving success," he wrote. "Please know that we would welcome the opportunity to work with you at a future date, and would be willing and able to travel to London or another location of your choosing for a second meeting. In the meantime, please keep us apprised of your decision-making, and certainly let us know if there is anything we can do to help."

By late May, Cassidy feared that the $5 million three-year payout it had banked on might be slipping away. Having heard nothing from me, Speed e-mailed to ask whether I still planned to come to Washington in June. If I were, "we would welcome the opportunity to meet again and discuss any of your firms [sic] projects [to] which we might be helpful. If you don't have plans to travel to the US, I will again express our willingness to meet you in London if that might be more advantageous to you and your schedule." His desperation was almost palpable.

I replied with an apologetic note. "I'm away from London until mid-June and it looks like the Washington trip has been pushed back until the beginning of July," I said. "I should have a precise date after I get back to London and will advise you then." That bought me all the time I needed, because the story was set to run in the July issue of *Harper's*, which would hit newsstands in mid-June, long before Speed would be expecting my arrival in Washington.

That was my final e-mail as Kenneth Case. The following month, APCO and Cassidy learned they'd been set up when *The Washington Post* called to get their reaction to the *Harper's* story, which was published under the title of "Their Men in Washington: Undercover with D.C.'s Lobbyists for Hire."

The story received a great deal of praise, but in short order, *Harper's* and I were also being strongly denounced—and not just by lobbyists, but by elements of the mainstream press as well.

SEVEN

Aftermath:

The Death of Undercover Reporting

GET READY FOR A SMALL ERUPTION ON K STREET, COURTESY OF Harper's magazine," *The Washington Post* said in an item that ran in June 2007, even before "Their Men in Washington: Undercover with D.C.'s Lobbyists for Hire" had hit newsstands. "The magazine's Ken Silverstein masqueraded as a person with an interest in the not-so-savory government of Turkmenistan and got some top lobbying firms to detail what they could do to improve its reputation."

The explosion was not long in coming.

Stung by the story, which got wide pickup on TV and radio and in the print press and the blogosphere, the lobbying firms struck back by trying, instinctually, to lie and spin their way out of the embarrassing situation. "We are surprised that a reporter would go to such extraordinary lengths to gather information in such a deceptive way that really isn't all that new or interesting," a Cassidy & Associates spokesman, Tom Alexander, said in a statement issued to *USA Today*.

But my favorite line from the statement was that the "context of the meeting described in the article was completely different from the context of the meeting requested." And what was the true context? I longed to ask Alexander. Had I actually asked Cassidy to lobby for Mother Teresa, which thereby explained why the firm had been so enthusiastic about winning the account? Apparently Cassidy hadn't known that the true client was the Turkmen government, and if it had, the firm would never, ever have considered the assignment.

Whereas Cassidy had the good sense to issue this statement and then retreat from the scene, APCO helpfully kept stirring the pot by denouncing me to media critics, issuing press releases, and generally protesting too much. (Dictators take note: Cassidy charges more than APCO, but it's smarter, too.) In a press release it posted on its corporate website, APCO claimed that it was never actually interested in winning the contract to work for Turkmenistan. "It is not uncommon for service businesses [*sic*] as ours to participate in a first, courtesy visit but to decline to work with a potential client afterwards—as APCO has done many times in the past," the statement said. "We ended the meeting [with the Maldon Group] politely and without any commitment or contractual relationship. There was never a further meeting, therefore no way for Silverstein to determine whether we would have taken the assignment."

No way, that is, other than Schumacher's flurry of plaintive e-mails after our meeting in Washington in which he anxiously sought to win the Turkmenistan deal, and his persistent effort to meet me in London before a decision was made by my alleged superiors about which lobbying firm to hire. The only reason there was no second meeting was that it was impossible for me to see Schumacher in London, as he had so eagerly proposed.

APCO's statement further claimed that there had been no need for me to go undercover to get information about APCO's activities, as it reveals everything in filings made under the Foreign Agents Registration Act and on its own website. And in "violation of recognized journalistic principles," I had never given APCO an opportunity to respond before publishing my story. (Neither APCO or Cassidy challenged the basic details of my account of our meetings, and for a good reason. An APCO spokesman told one interviewer that he had "inferred from the precise and accurate retelling of the APCO meeting that either Silverstein or the mysterious Ricardo might have surreptitiously recorded the session.")

APCO and Cassidy got additional backing from Kathy Cripps of the Council of Public Relations Firms (of which APCO is a member). In a letter to *Harper's* she said my story displayed "the tawdry side of investigative journalism" and that the magazine and I needed to "reassess [our] current standards of reporting." Where was Cripps when poor old Ivy Lee needed her? Had it been the 1930s and the offices of Lee I had infiltrated, one could easily imagine Cripps denouncing me for my "tawdry" exposure of the Führer's man. There was indeed a party here who needed to take a good, hard look in the mirror.

Indeed, a section of Cripps's letter read as if it had been drafted by Lee. "We always tell our clients that honesty is the best policy," the latter wrote in a 1906 statement of principles. "Our plan is, frankly and openly, on behalf of business concerns and public institutions, to supply the press and the public of the United States prompt and accurate information concerning subjects which it is of value and interest to the public to know about." Fast forward to 2007. "[The] Council of Public Relations Firms encourages members to embrace their responsibilities to foster open dialogue and transparent behavior," Cripps wrote to *Harper's*. "Not only is this in the public interest and the right thing to do but it is also critical for establishing credibility with potential audiences and constituencies."

Further support, though probably not exactly the type the two firms were looking for, came from a small-fry Washington lobbyist named Laurence Socci. In a self-serving and patently obvious effort to woo dictators to his firm, Socci was quoted defending his profession in several news stories about the controversy. The gist of his argument was laid out in slightly more detail in an e-mail he sent to me. "As a lawyer, I would have no problem representing a rapist or child molester, although I despise both crimes," he wrote. "To me, it's not a personal reflection that I would stoop so low [as] to represent these types of clients. It's a job that I do to put food on the table and care for my family. As a lawyer, I believe that everyone deserves competent representation. As a lobbyist, I believe that everyone deserves an opportunity to be heard before Members of Congress. As I have often said, I would represent the devil himself for the right price—it's not personal, just business."

Though starkly put, Socci's comparison of lobbyists to defense attorneys is in fact the most common defense offered by lobbyists who work for foreign despots. But there are of course some rather striking distinctions here. Lawyers represent clients who may or may not be guilty, and when the evidence against them is clear, the clients almost always go to prison. Lobbyists for dictators are working for people whose crimes are generally documented beyond dispute, and when they succeed, they enhance their clients' grip on power and ability to continue oppressing their citizens and pillaging the national treasury. The only people at risk of going to jail are political dissidents opposing the dictator clients.

The public response to the story was overwhelming, and almost entirely positive. A lot of people, it seemed, just didn't approve of lobby shops doing image enhancement work for dictators. Among the hundreds of e-mails I received came one from a person who urged that I never apologize for "misrepresenting yourself to a pack of thugs . . . especially when misrepresentation is their own stock in trade!" Perhaps the most gratifying recognition was that the story helped inspire a *Doonesbury* series in which "Duke" and his son are portrayed as Beltway lobbyists who go to work for the dictator ruling "Berzerkistan."

"Dad, the billings from our new rogue regime division have been phenomenal," the son tells Duke. "Major kudos!"

"I have to say, even I'm a bit surprised how well I seem to represent dictators," comes the reply. "Who knew I'd be so good at framing evil?"

I also received numerous supportive e-mails from journalists, including one from an editor at a major mainstream outlet who said he had photocopied and distributed my story to a number of reporters who worked for him:

Several staffers told me that your piece was an eye opener about how Washington really works, and illuminated how the issues and events . . . and press releases they regularly report on materialize in the first place. Certainly, as your critics suggest, the fact that lobbying exists is not "news"— but given how sophisticated it, and the spin-machine in general, has become, an article like yours is imperative for journalists . . . to keep in mind. We are usually so wrapped up in getting the daily stories out that we don't have as much time as we'd like to pause and reflect—and report some more—on the interests being served by speeches, trade agreements, regulatory changes and legislative proposals.

The response from the lobbying and public relations trade press was less friendly, though not wholly hostile. *PRWeek,* the industry's premier journal, granted me an interview to lay out my case, then ran a neutral story that said the Turkmenistan article had "set up a heated debate about the nature of lobbying work with foreign governments, as well as journalistic ethics and practices."

As part of its counterattack, APCO pitched a number of media critics to write about my shady ethics, though not always terribly successfully. "What Silverstein uncovered was disgusting," Edward Wasserman, a Knight professor in journalism at Washington and Lee University, wrote in *The Miami Herald* after hearing from APCO. "We're talking about regimes that are robbing their people and lavishing a portion of their plunder on U.S. lobbyists whose entire mission is to enable them to continue their thieving. . . . Deception is a nasty business, and I respect those who say it's never justified. But was Silverstein the trickster we should be worried about in this affair?"

APCO also sought support from Doug Fisher, a longtime print and broadcast reporter who now teaches journalism at the University of South Carolina and who writes a blog called Common Sense Journalism. Fisher did criticize me, primarily for failing to respond adequately to the ethics controversy on the *Harper's* website, but said, "Silverstein has pulled just a little bit of the covers off the sordid underbelly of Washington lobbying. . . . Do I have a problem with Silverstein's going under cover? No, because I doubt there was any other way to get the insight he did."

APCO had better luck with Howard Kurtz, the media columnist for *The Washington Post* and host of CNN's *Reliable Sources*. And that pointed to a fabulous bit of irony, namely that while I did receive a fair amount of criticism about the piece, the most intense (other than from the lobbyists themselves) came from Beltway reporters and pundits. For them, my story prompted a moral crisis. They just couldn't figure out whether it was worse for me to have tricked the lobbyists or for the lobbyists to have proposed a whitewash campaign for the Turkmen regime.

I'd never been a fan of Kurtz, who has become the nation's leading journalism cop. He's a reliable champion of the "balanced" coverage that plagues American journalism and which leads to utterly spineless reporting with no edge. The idea seems to be that journalists are allowed to go out to report, but when it comes time to write, we are expected to turn our brains off and repeat the spin from both sides. God forbid we should attempt to fairly assess what we see with our own eyes. "Balanced" is not fair, it's just an easy way of avoiding real reporting (as well as charges of bias) and shirking our responsibility to inform readers.

I'd worked at the *Los Angeles Times* as an investigative reporter for several years and had periodically been frustrated by the limits of the "balanced" approach. One example came in the fall of 2004, just before the presidential election between George Bush and John Kerry, when I traveled to the battleground state of Missouri to write about Democratic efforts to mobilize African American voters and possible GOP attempts to suppress the vote in St. Louis and other heavily Democratic areas. This was especially notable because the Justice Department found that during the 2000 presidential election, huge numbers of African Americans in St. Louis had been improperly turned away from the polls.

Democrats in Missouri were particularly critical of Mis-

souri's Republican secretary of state, Matt Blunt. He was supposed to ensure the impartiality of the vote, but there were signs
that he was acting in a partisan manner—no surprise, since
Blunt was active in the Bush-Cheney reelection campaign. In
July 2004, three months before I arrived in St. Louis, *The New
York Times* had run an editorial about Blunt, titled "An Umpire
Takes Sides," which said he was a prime example of "a major flaw
in the American electoral system," namely that "the top election
officers in most states are men and women who are publicly
rooting for the Democratic or Republican side." To take just one
example, Blunt had sought to block early voting in St. Louis.
That policy, which is now widely employed in the United States,
allows senior citizens and others who might have a hard time
getting out on Election Day to cast their ballots in advance of the
actual vote.

Meanwhile, some Republican officials were accusing the
Democrats of wholesale fraud. Democratic voter registration
groups, I was told while in St. Louis, had submitted hundreds of
voter applications with invalid names, including the names of
people who were dead. Yet there was no evidence to suggest that
large numbers of people using fake names were going to turn
out to vote come Election Day, and certainly not in numbers
large enough to influence the outcome. There had been "no intent to commit fraud" by Democratic groups, Mike Leuken, a Republican on the St. Louis Board of Elections, told me, adding that
the voter rolls were "generally in good shape."

Based on what I'd seen, I filed a 2,500-word story that focused on the more serious issues raised by the Democratic side.
Soon, though, I was told that the *Los Angeles Times* had sent reporters to three other states and that my findings would be in-
corporated into a broad national story about how during the
run-up to the election, each side was accusing the other of cheat-

ing. The story ran on October 26, 2004, under the headline "Partisan Suspicions Run High in Swing States; Democrats say the GOP aims to disenfranchise the poor and minorities. Republicans counter with claims of voter registration fraud."

"Everywhere, it seems, the presidential campaign is awash in reports of fraud, dirty tricks and intimidation," the *Times* breathlessly reported. The story went on to discuss how "Democrats and Republicans seem convinced their opponents are bent on stealing the election," described the "extraordinarily rancorous and mistrustful atmosphere that pervades battleground states in the final days of the presidential campaign," and suggested that the whole thing might be nothing more than paranoid, overheated complaints by party hacks. "Each side sees the Nov. 2 balloting as a critical choice between clashing values and ideas about where the country should be heading," read the story. "Each state, precinct and volunteer organization is convinced its efforts alone stand between the nation and a catastrophic miscarriage of electoral justice." The 2,500 words that I'd filed had been reduced to a small section that was roughly divided between charges and countercharges from Democrats and Republicans.

In other words, we had sent four reporters to four states and spent untold thousands of dollars to produce a story that said absolutely nothing. Our story was perfectly balanced, perfectly neutral, and perfectly useless.

Another case in point was the *Post*'s own massive series on Cassidy & Associates (discussed in the last chapter), which came in with a whimper in March of 2007 and went out with a whimper five weeks later. It uncovered a few choice anecdotes about the firm but was watered down with so much "he said, she said" journalism that it seemed to have no point of view, narrative, or even central argument. It was a masterpiece of Howard Kurtz–

style journalism, and predictably was little commented upon and created no impact.

So it was no surprise when Kurtz proved to be less concerned by the lobbyists' ability to manipulate public and political opinion than by my use of undercover journalism. "When you use lying and cheating to get a story, even a really juicy story, it raises as many questions about the journalist as his target," he said in a *Reliable Sources* commentary.

A number of inside-the-Beltway critics wrote that my story was old news—hardly worth reporting at all. What I had found, summarized a post on the CBS News website, was that lobbyists "occasionally tuck their conscience in the attic for a check. Which is something they've been doing for the better part of the last 100 years." I can see the point. Corrupt lobbyists have been around forever, sort of like poor people—and who wants to read about them? In fact, you won't see much in American newspapers about poverty, unless there's a "hook." After Hurricane Katrina there was all sorts of media soul-searching about the plight of the poor and how the press had ignored the topic. It was so serious that Anderson Cooper shed tears. But how many articles and TV specials about American poverty have you seen recently? I guess we'll have to wait for another natural disaster to be reminded of that boring subject.

I can't say I was utterly surprised by the criticism, especially of undercover journalism. Some major media organizations allow reporters, in principle, to employ it—assuming the story in question is deemed vital to the public interest and cannot be obtained through more conventional means—but very few practice it anymore. And that's unfortunate, because there's a long tradition of sting operations in American journalism, dating back at least to the 1880s, when Nellie Bly pretended to be insane in order to reveal the atrocious treatment of inmates at the

Women's Lunatic Asylum on Blackwell's Island in New York City.

Such tactics were always controversial but widely practiced until relatively recently. During the 1970s, *60 Minutes* gained fame for its use of sting stories, and the *Chicago Tribune* won several Pulitzer Prizes with undercover reporting. One came in 1971, when reporter William Jones got a job as an ambulance driver and showed that poor patients who didn't pay drivers didn't get taken to the hospital. The *Tribune*'s William Gaines won two Pulitzers, once for going undercover as a bill collector and reporting on the abusive tactics they employed, and a second time for getting a job as a janitor at a hospital and exposing poor conditions there. In his 2007 essay about the decline of undercover reporting, Gaines said the stories "were shocking in a city where it takes a lot to shock people," and wrote that "readers responded to us favorably, the journalism community gave us awards, and even Congress loved us."

In the late 1970s, the *Chicago Sun-Times* bought its own tavern, the Mirage, and exposed (in a twenty-five-part series) gross corruption on the part of city inspectors—such as the fire inspector who agreed to ignore exposed electrical wiring for a mere ten-dollar payoff. The series was a smash hit with the public, but by then undercover reporting was becoming unpopular within the journalism establishment itself. The Mirage sting was considered to be a strong favorite to win a Pulitzer in 1978, but it was an also-ran. Several prominent newspaper officials, including Ben Bradlee, *The Washington Post*'s executive editor at the time of Watergate, reportedly opposed awarding the *Sun-Times* the prize because of its use of deception.

That was a crushing blow to undercover reporting, because, as anyone who has spent any time around a big-city newspaper knows, vast effort is spent in pursuit of the Pulitzer and other

big prizes. Once it became clear that undercover stings had little chance of winning such prizes, editors had little incentive to commission such work.

Gaines himself later became ambivalent about undercover reporting. "I joke that, if undercover reporting comes back in style, I will be ready with my mop and bucket," he wrote in his essay. "I say that safely because I know it will not return. It was a unique chapter in journalism that exposed wrongdoing and waste and got protection for victims of fraud." Given that wrongdoing, waste, and fraud were hardly unique to the 1970s and are alive and well today, I don't see what should make undercover reporting out of bounds currently.

Yet today, it's almost impossible to imagine a mainstream media outlet undertaking a major undercover investigation. That's partly a result of the 1997 verdict against ABC News in the Food Lion case. The TV network accused Food Lion of selling cheese that had been gnawed on by rats as well as spoiled meat and fish that had been doused with bleach to cover up its rancid smell. But even though the grocery chain never denied the allegations in court, it successfully sued ABC for fraud—arguing that the reporters only made those discoveries after getting jobs at Food Lion by lying on their résumés. In other words, the fact that their reporting was accurate was no longer a defense. ABC News chairman Roone Arledge wrote a *New York Times* op-ed piece defending undercover journalism, saying that his network's reporters had previously exposed fraud and abuse at day care centers, hospitals, and government health programs. "Not one of the institutions we investigated would have volunteered to tell all if a reporter had showed up with a camera," he wrote.

The decline of undercover reporting—and of investigative reporting in general—also reflects, in part, the increasing conservatism and cautiousness of the media, especially the smug,

high-end Washington press corps. As reporters have grown more socially prominent during the last several decades, they've become part of the very power structure that they're supposed to be tracking and scrutinizing. R. W. Apple, the late *New York Times* reporter, well illustrated the matter. A close friend of super-lobbyists such as Robert Strauss and Anne Wexler, he once described himself (in an interview with Kurtz) as an "establishment" type of guy. If former top government officials like Lawrence Eagleburger or Zbigniew Brzezinski were to tell Apple that a story he was working on was "a lot of crap," he'd be "hesitant to put it forward," he said. Just what we need in American journalism: reporters who vet stories with leading members of the political establishment.

Ben Bradlee has noted that reporters have become far more conservative in recent years. "There's a very good reason for that," he once explained. "They get paid a hell of a lot better. It's hard to be conservative on $75 a week, but [at] seventy-five grand, you begin to think of the kids and the bank account and the IRA."

Indeed, take a look at the 2008 Social List of *Washington Life,* which bills itself as the city's "premier luxury-lifestyle magazine." The Social List "is Washington's answer to the old-world *Almanach de Gotha,* that weighty tome across whose 18th-century pages the sovereign families of Europe bled blue," says a pompous note from Editor in Chief Nancy Bagley that is beyond satire. "We take high society for its modern translation—an institution which gives a bit of structure (not to mention flawless poise, exquisite etiquette and gracious lifestyle) to social order." Scattered among the 2008 list, along with government officials, business executives, lobbyists, and foreign ambassadors and royalty (among them, Their Imperial Highnesses Prince and Princess Reza Pahlavi, son and daughter-in-law of the former

Shah of Iran), are numerous Beltway media celebrities: CBS cor-
respondent Riva Braver (and her husband, the lawyer Robert Bar-
nett, whose clients include Lynne Cheney, wife of the vice
president, both of whom are on the list as well); James Carney of
Time magazine and his wife, Claire Shipman of ABC; Thomas
Friedman of *The New York Times* (and his wife, the daughter of a
real estate tycoon whose family assets in 2007 were estimated by
Forbes to be $4.1 billion, and with whom he shares an 11,400-
square-foot, $9.3 million home); David Gregory of NBC (and his
wife, Beth Wilkinson, a top Washington lawyer and executive at
Fannie Mae)—the list goes on and on.

The cloying, incestuous relationship between the high-end
press and the political establishment has been starkly revealed
during recent dinners of the White House Correspondents' Association (WHCA), which sponsors an annual gathering of the nation's political and media elites. Stephen Colbert of Comedy
Central's *Colbert Report* keynoted the 2006 event, and he took
some pointed shots at President Bush. "I stand by this man, because he stands for things," Colbert said of Bush, who was in attendance. "Not only *for* things, he stands *on* things—things like
aircraft carriers and rubble and recently flooded city squares.
And that sends a strong message, that no matter what happens
to America, she will always rebound with the most powerfully
staged photo ops in the world."

Worse still, Colbert saved his most withering remarks for
the media. "Let's review the rules," he told the assembled digni-
taries. "Here's how it works: The president makes decisions. He's
the decider. The press secretary announces those decisions, and
you people of the press type those decisions down. Make, announce, type. Just put 'em through spell-check and go home. Get
to know your family again. Make love to your wife. Write that
novel you got kicking around in your head. You know, the one

about the intrepid Washington reporter with the courage to stand up to the administration. You know—fiction!"

The media was not amused. Richard Cohen of *The Washington Post* wrote a column about Colbert's performance with the headline "So Not Funny." Colbert, wrote Cohen, was "not just a failure as a comedian but rude," as well as someone "representative of what too often passes for political courage."

And so the following year, the event's planners ensured that the night would be entirely free of controversy by hiring as emcee Rich Little, best known (decades ago) for his bland, apolitical comedy and impersonations of President Richard Nixon. (A number of other performers had declined offers to host the dinner, and Robin Williams was reportedly vetoed when his agent warned that he might, like Colbert, be critical of President Bush.) "Bob Hope Sadly Too Dead to Headline WHCA Dinner," ran the droll headline of a story about Little's hiring on the website Wonkette.

Little's performance at the dinner was every bit as dull as one would have expected. He avoided jokes about then current political issues, and his "edgiest" remarks made fun of Bush's propensity to mangle the English language, such as a crack about this "warathon thing against all extreministic fractions." What a riot. But the organizers, at least, were satisfied. "Regardless of what you think of Rich Little, he was really excited to do this," Steve Scully, a senior executive producer of C-SPAN and the president of the association, said. "And the President and Mrs. Bush—they really loved it."

I'm willing to debate the merits of my piece, but the carping from the Washington press corps was hard to stomach. As a class, they value politeness over honesty and believe that being "balanced" means giving the same weight to a lie as you give to the truth. I'll take Nellie Bly any day. (Despite believing that a good slice of the Washington press corps is far too close to the political elite, I would note here that there is still plenty of brilliant journalism being done today, much of it in the mainstream media.)

In terms of the relevant journalism ethics, I agree that undercover reporting should be used sparingly, and there are valid arguments to be made as to when it is appropriate. But I'm confident my use of it in the case of Turkmeniscam was legitimate. There was a significant public interest involved, particularly given Congress's unfulfilled promise to crack down on lobbyists in the aftermath of the Jack Abramoff scandal. I was able to gain an inside glimpse into a secretive culture of professional spinners only by dissembling in turn. Could I have extracted the same information and insight with more conventional journalistic methods? Impossible. And while I could have taken a number of different approaches, none would have yielded as revealing a story or had the same impact.

As to not calling APCO or Cassidy for comment, I had a few reasons. First, while it would have been unlikely, I feared a prepublication legal threat to block the story. Second, and this seemed a far bigger risk, the *Harper's* publication schedule is such that calling the firms for comment would have given the lobbyists, who are professional spinners, more than a month to counterattack before the story hit newsstands.

Indeed, I'd had a previous experience with *The Washington Post* that made me particularly skeptical of giving the lobbyists so much time to maneuver. Back in 1998, I had written a story for *Mother Jones* magazine about a lobbying campaign mounted by Anne Wexler on behalf of a corporate coalition called USA*Engage, which was seeking to restrict the use of American economic sanctions on dictatorial regimes. The piece was based on several boxes of sensitive internal documents from Wexler's office that were turned over to me by a particularly generous source. But Wexler had great success in defusing the PR fallout with the help of Bill McAllister, then a reporter with the *Post.*

Just after the story ran, he called Wexler, who told him that the documents I'd cited were "standard stuff" and that many had been simply downloaded from the USA*Engage website. It was an obvious lie, but McAllister printed it anyway, apparently without bothering to consult the website, where he would not have found any of the documents from my story. He also ran with an allegation by Wexler that documents that had not been on the website might possibly have been obtained by a hacker, which implied that I had possibly engaged in criminal conduct or, at best, been in cahoots with someone who had engaged in criminal conduct. (McAllister never called me for comment, though for some reason Kurtz didn't seem troubled in that particular instance. I left him a message complaining about McAllister's story, but never heard back.)

Finally, my story was, after all, an undercover sting. I had disclosed my deceptions clearly in the piece I wrote (whereas the lobbyists I met boasted of how they were able to fly under the radar in seeking to shape U.S. foreign policy). If readers felt uncomfortable with my methods, they were free to dismiss my findings. And what was I going to ask APCO and Cassidy? "Would you work for a Stalinist dictatorship if offered enough money?" That had already been answered. The only outstanding question that I had for the lobbyists was this: How do you look yourself in the mirror?

I'm comfortable comparing my ethics in setting up and carrying out the sting to the ethics of lobbyists who were so willing to represent and whitewash the record of a Stalinist dictatorship. The Turkmeniscam sting was not a matter of entrapping Boy Scouts by putting a wallet on the ground. If the firms hadn't been blinded by greed and viewed the Maldon Group as a big, glowing sack of money, they would never have been taken in by my flimsy cover story.

EVERY SO OFTEN, PUBLIC OUTRAGE COMPELS CONGRESS TO MAKE A show of its determination to "clean up" Washington. Back in the mid-1990s, the new Republican Congress, which swept aside more than forty years of Democratic control, vowed to crack down on corruption and special interests. It imposed a set of sweeping reforms, including a fifty-dollar limit on lobbyist-sponsored meals and gifts. "A year after Federal lawmakers imposed on themselves one of the most restrictive codes of conduct ever and on the eve of the start of the first full Congress to live under those regulations, members of the House and Senate are starting to feel the full bite," *The New York Times* reported in January 1997.

The *Times* said that the tough new rules had "altered the traditional way of doing business in the nation's capital," bewildered some groups seeking "to gain access and cull favors from the power brokers on Capitol Hill," and threatened the livelihood of restaurants favored by politicians. "Even an updated Emily Post might have trouble directing one around the pitfalls of [the new] rules," the newspaper said. Meanwhile, lawmakers consulted by the *Times* complained that the gift ban had had "a chilling effect"; during the previous Christmas season, members of Congress who had been invited to elaborate parties even had to determine with hosts who was paying for the event before they could confirm their attendance.

The chill soon thawed. By late 1997, we now know, lobbyists and businessmen were routinely treating Duke Cunningham to lavish meals at the Capital Grille. Jack Abramoff was soon run-

ning amok as well, offering on-the-house wining and dining to
lawmakers at his restaurant Signatures. Things went downhill
from there. In 2005, Mitchell Wade, one of the businessmen subsequently revealed to have bribed Cunningham, paid for a
$2,800 meal with then Congresswoman Katherine Harris at Cit-
ronelle, located in Georgetown's Latham Hotel and deemed to be
"one of the world's most exciting restaurants" by *Condé Nast
Traveler.* When caught, Harris claimed that she'd simply forgotten to contribute to the check, and that Wade had done most of
the damage. "Do I look like I ate twenty-eight hundred dollars in
one sitting?" she asked. "I always get a couple of appetizers and
something to drink."

These may have been extreme cases, but freebies for members of Congress from lobbyists had again become standard operating procedure. At the trial of Brent Wilkes, Capital Grille
waiter Clifford Horsfall was put on the stand. During questioning by Wilkes's attorney, he said that he could not recall a single
time during his thirteen years on the job that a congressman had
picked up the tab when dining with lobbyists.

These sorts of abuses led to the election of the new Democratic Congress, which commenced work in 2007 with calls to
curb the influence of lobbyists. In August, Congress passed legislation by overwhelming margins—411–8 in the House and
83–14 in the Senate—that demanded "unprecedented disclosure of how lobbyists interact with lawmakers," reported *The
Wall Street Journal.* "Months in the making, the measure has
been a major priority following the scandals of the previous,
Republican-controlled Congress and represents the most ambitious effort to tighten ethics rules in a decade." In September,
President Bush signed the bill into law and congratulated lawmakers for making progress toward strengthening "ethical standards that govern lobbying activities."

New rules approved by Congress included a flat-out prohibition on lobbyists' treating lawmakers to meals and trips; restrictions on the use of corporate jets by members of Congress; a rule that barred former lawmakers from directly lobbying their old colleagues for two years after retiring, twice the previous standard; and various steps designed to reduce pork-barreling and make the earmarking process more transparent. Indeed, some wondered whether the whole ethics craze had gotten out of hand. "Things have gone so far in the nation's capital that ethics is getting in the way of religion," *The Washington Post* reported in the fall of 2007, in an article that bore eerie similarity to the *New York Times* article published almost exactly a decade earlier in the aftermath of the mid-1990s ethics reform bill. It told the tale of a lobbyist who had stopped serving pastries at a weekly Bible session he hosted that was widely attended by congressional aides. The reason: pastry came perilously close to constituting a meal, which would violate the new law's ban on gifts to members of Congress or staffers.

Yet abundant signs from the outset suggested that the new ethics rules' impact wouldn't be nearly so drastic. Indeed, on September 14, the very day that Bush signed the bill into law, a number of top lobbyists sent out an invitation for a fund-raising luncheon for Pete Olson, a Texas Republican who was planning a congressional run. The fund-raiser was held at the Independence Avenue townhouse of Williams & Jensen, a top lobbying firm whose clients include a number of big energy and pharmaceutical firms, as well as the U.S. Chamber of Commerce. The lobbyists hosting the affair included former congressman Greg Laughlin; John Runyan, who works for International Paper; and Jeff Munk, who previously helped raise money for Tom DeLay.

And so went life in post-Abramoff Washington. The new ethics rules specified that members of Congress could no longer travel on a lobbyist's dime, yet lawmakers were still free to host and sponsor vacation-style fund-raisers that lobbyists and other big donors paid for through their attendance. A number of Washington influence peddlers flew to Alaska over the summer of 2007 to join Senator Ted Stevens of Alaska on a fishing/fund-raising trip to Prince of Wales Island. Later in the year lobbyists and other big donors holed up with Senator Mel Martinez at the private Gilchrist Club, spread across twenty-three thousand acres of Florida woodlands, for a weekend of quail and pheasant hunting.

The New York Times documented a catalog of lawmaker-lobbyist outings, including a California wine-tasting tour, golf tournaments, a concert by the Who, and excursions to Disney World and South Beach. "Lobbyists and fund-raisers say such trips are becoming increasingly popular, partly as a quirky consequence of the new ethics rules," the newspaper said. "Lobbyists say that the rules might even increase the volume of contributions flowing to Congress from K Street."

Nor did the new ethics rules slow the revolving door between Congress and the private sector. "Ka-ching!" began a November 2007 story in *Politico*. "It's Senate Minority Whip Trent Lott's turn to trade in his U.S. Capitol pin for cold hard cash on K Street." Lott had just unexpectedly announced his resignation from Congress—to avoid, it soon became clear, the new two-year ban on lobbying former colleagues—and speculation was already rife that he would start a lobbying firm with former Louisiana Democratic senator John Breaux, who was then at Patton Boggs. "The only real question," one lobbyist said of a potential Lott-Breaux partnership, "would be whether they would hire Brinks to bring in the money every day."

In January 2008 came the inevitable confirmation: The Brinks Job was indeed on.

And what about pork? House Speaker Nancy Pelosi had promised that earmarking would be drastically reduced, but it didn't quite work out as well as she had vowed. During 2007, according to Taxpayers for Common Sense, congressional representatives secured more than 11,000 earmarks worth $15 billion. Congressman John Murtha retained his title of House Pork King, racking up $162 million in earmarks for his Pennsylvania district. "The Murtha operation—which has become a model for other entrepreneurial lawmakers—is a gross example of quid pro quo Washington," said a *New York Times* editorial in January 2008. "Every one of the 26 beneficiaries of Mr. Murtha's earmarks in last year's defense budget made contributions to his campaign kitty, a total of $413,250, according to the newspaper Roll Call." Meanwhile, David Morrison, Murtha's staff director at the Defense Appropriations Subcommittee, moved through the revolving door as well. The same month he signed on with the Podesta Group lobbying firm, where he was made head of the national security and international practice area.

There were other discouraging news reports in January. "Congressional Crackdown on Lobbying Is Already Showing Cracks," said a *Times* story, which cited Congress's "creative interpretations of the new rules." It said, in agreeing with watchdog groups that a House proposal to create a new ethics panel was far too weak, that "strict regulations are useless without strict enforcement."

The Washington Post reported on the fate of a new rule that flatly prohibited lobbyists from hosting parties to honor lawmakers at presidential conventions. "The House ethics committee, in its wisdom, issued an interpretation of the new law last month that leaves little of it intact," the newspaper said in an editorial. Among other things, the ethics panel had determined that only parties honoring a "specific member" would be prohibited; celebrations paying homage to more than one lawmaker wouldn't be covered, which amounted to a rather broad loophole. Furthermore, only parties paid for "directly" by lobbyists would be outlawed, but private groups could still solicit money from lobbyists and use it to sponsor convention fetes. "Hard to imagine a clearer road map for lobbyists interested in getting around the intent of the new law," the *Post* concluded. In April 2008, a Washington watchdog group reported that Washington lobbying firms had received a record-setting $2.8 billion in fees the previous year. That was up $200 million, nearly 8 percent, from 2006.

Meanwhile, presidential candidates from both parties were loudly attacking lobbyists yet quietly using them to raise the money they needed for the 2008 campaign. By January, according to Public Citizen, the leading candidates still in the race had 142 lobbyists as "bundlers," the term for the very biggest fundraisers who round up money for campaigns. That was six more than the number of lobbyist-bundlers during the entire 2004 campaign. Republican John McCain, his party's eventual nominee, led the field by far with fifty-nine, while Hillary Clinton had twenty lobbyist-bundlers and Barack Obama had ten. Lobbyists were playing key roles elsewhere as well. Richard Davis, one of the most powerful telecommunications lobbyists in town, was the McCain campaign chairman. Lobbyist Janice Enright was serving as the treasurer of HillPAC, one of Clinton's political committees.

There was controversy involving foreign lobbyists, too. In April 2008, Hillary Clinton's chief presidential campaign strategist, Mark Penn, resigned after it was revealed that he had met with Colombian government officials who were looking to build congressional support for a free-trade agreement that Clinton explicitly opposed. Penn held the meetings in his role as CEO of

Burson-Marsteller Worldwide, the lobbying and PR giant. The following month, Doug Goodyear, who had been picked by Mc-Cain's campaign to run the 2008 GOP convention in Minneapolis, resigned after it was reported that the lobbying firm he headed had once represented the military dictatorship in Burma. Goodyear's firm, called the DCI Group, had received $348,000 in 2002 to "begin a dialogue of political reconciliation" between the regime and the U.S. government.

TO CATCH A GLIMPSE OF HOW WASHINGTON WORKS, STAND NEAR THE Capitol South metro station around 6:30 P.M. on weeknights when Congress is in session. You'll frequently see a stream of members, staffers, and their acquaintances, in groups of twos, threes, and fours, fanning out across the city. The stream soon divides, with some branches flowing toward nearby destinations such as the Capitol Hill Club, a Republican haven located across the street from the Rayburn House Office Building, or the cavernous Charlie Palmer Steak, which sits on the ground floor of a ten-story building that houses the offices of various lobbying groups and political operatives. (Sitting atop a corridor of marble that runs down the dining room at Charlie Palmer's is a vast wine cube, which holds thirty-five hundred bottles.) Other options popular among the political class include the Oceanaire Seafood Room, known far and wide for its amazing crab cakes; the Caucus Room just off Pennsylvania Avenue, whose owners include Democratic lobbyist Tommy Boggs and former Republican National Committee chairman and current Mississippi governor Haley Barbour; and beef shrines such as Sam & Harry's downtown, Morton's in Georgetown, or the Capital Grille.

Most Americans could not afford to eat at these or other restaurants popular with the political class. The price of an appetizer alone—such as the $15.95 lobster mac-and-cheese at Oceanaire or the $18 lobster, crab, and shrimp cocktail at the Capitol Hill Club (why settle for one when you can have all three?)—is daunting. The à la carte entrées begin at the low end with items like the stuffed rabbit loin at a chic Capitol Hill eatery called Bistro Bis ($29.50), move up to the signature porterhouse at the Capital Grille ($41) or the double prime rib at Morton's ($43), and for the truly memorable occasion climb to $20 per ounce (5-ounce minimum) for the Kobe strip steak at Charlie Palmer's. With drinks, dessert, and a tip, a meal for two can easily run into the hundreds of dollars.

Yet these are the everyday haunts of our elected leaders. Between 2005 and late 2007, House members used $5.4 million in campaign money alone to dine at ten of Washington's priciest restaurants, according to figures compiled by the Center for Responsive Politics. Note that this does not even include senators, who typically spend even more than their colleagues in the lower chamber; but because senators are not required to file disclosure forms electronically, categorizing their expenses with any specificity is a nearly impossible task.

And who is dining with our lawmakers? You may see a tourist here and there craning his neck to try to spot a political luminary, but most customers at the capital's high-end establishments are on an expense account of one sort or another. It's a small club, and other than political officials, most of the diners are lobbyists, PR flacks, consultants, fund-raisers, and other assorted hangers-on whose living depends on access to them.

Tom Quinn, a well-connected Democratic lobbyist in town— during the 2008 presidential primaries he supported Hillary Clinton, but he also raised money for longtime friends Christopher Dodd and Joe Biden—goes out for drinks or dinner just about every night. "I know a lot of people, and there are a few ladies who think I'm a nice guy," he said with a wink over lunch one afternoon at Zola, another popular political hangout. "It's a company town. In New York you talk about the market, in Los Angeles about the movie business, and here it's politics and public policy." Quinn invariably runs into members of Congress and staffers as he makes his rounds, so a night on the town is part play and part work. "It's not influence that's being traded," he said of his evening rounds, "it's information: what's going to move the needle on a bill, what the schedule is, understanding some staff director's personality—there are a million different aspects. A lot of what I do is about knowledge, experience, and procedures. Information is part of the game."

During the period of GOP rule, the Capital Grille, which at Pennsylvania Avenue and Sixth Street sits in the reflected glow of the Capitol dome, was perhaps the most popular restaurant in town for Republican insiders. The restaurant opened in 1994, the year that Newt Gingrich led the GOP takeover of Congress, and on its opening night handed out a hundred thousand dollars' worth of free food and drink to legislators. "It might as well be part of the Capitol complex," *The Hill* newspaper remarked in 2004, "like the Russell Senate Office Building or the Rayburn House Office Building, since you're likely to run into almost as many members of Congress and staffers at the Capital Grille as you do on Capitol Hill."

Business reportedly dropped off when the Democrats took charge again in 2006, but it remained one of the best spots in town to hobnob with members of Congress and their entourages. When I visited the Capital Grille one night last fall, three SUVs were idling out front for lawmakers who were finishing up inside. As I walked toward the revolving front door, Representative Charles Rangel (D-NY), head of the House Ways and Means Committee, was walking out. A man just in front of me—likely a lobbyist, given his power suit, briefcase, and Bluetooth earpiece—immediately accosted Rangel, furiously shaking his hand, and the two men struck up a short but friendly conversation. After Rangel stepped into his waiting car (license plate NYREP 15), the man turned to me, eyes afire, and exclaimed, "He's da man!"

Inside, just past a window display of aged beef slabs hanging like holy relics, the first thing one sees is a wall of wine lockers, their owners' names engraved on brass plaques. Duke Cunningham and his former friends Wilkes and Wade used to have lockers here. Those whose names still grace lockers include Jeffrey Shockey, a top aide to Republican congressman Jerry Lewis, who while previously working as a lobbyist had remarkable success at winning earmarks from Lewis's Appropriations Committee, and Ann Eppard, who flourished as a lobbyist despite having pled guilty in 1999 to taking payoffs while working for a Republican congressman, Bud Shuster, who had been a perennial powerhouse on the House Transportation Committee. (Eppard's locker is maintained in memoriam.)

In the bar just beyond, an assortment of politicos can inevitably be found milling about. On one night in October 2007, I saw Terry Nelson, who had served until the summer as John McCain's presidential campaign manager, strolling through toward the dining room; William Pickle, the recently retired Senate sergeant at arms, moving from stool to stool, chatting with acquaintances; and a dapper Arthur Wu, the Republican staff director of the House Veterans' Affairs Oversight and Investigations Subcommittee, who stood at center stage with a big smile and glass in hand. Senator Norm Coleman of Minnesota, who had dropped by after a fund-raiser held in his honor earlier in the evening at the U.S. Chamber of Commerce town house, sipped from a drink while chatting with Matthew Brooks, head of the Republican Jewish Coalition.

On another night, I shared drinks with several lobbyists who meet regularly at the Grille. "They decided to criminalize everything," one said, referring to the ban on lobbyists' buying meals for lawmakers. "My reaction is, 'Have a good life.' It's not going to hurt me, I already know people, but it's going to make it hard for those who are new [at lobbying] and are trying to build personal relationships." One of our tablemates was also untroubled. "So far, it's saved me a lot of money," he said. "But I'm not sure what's going to happen in the long run. When they lowered the speed limit to fifty-five, everyone paid attention for six months. Then they started driving seventy again."

As we chatted, conservative Democratic senator Ben Nelson came into the bar from the dining room and struck up a conversation with two men, while several suitors lined up to wait their turn. Also on hand was Edwina Rogers, a lobbyist and the wife of Republican power broker Ed Rogers, who along with a friend was enjoying a night on the town that still included a planned stop at Georgetown's Café Milano. Rogers, whose freewheeling style seemed hard to square with her role as a conservative strategist and former Bush White House aide at the National Economic Council, was engaged in conversation with someone whom she identified to me, moments later, as an important committee staffer. The topic wasn't hard to discern.

"You need to make Rick an offer of at least three times what he's making now," the man told Rogers.

"Let's get together Thursday at Charlie Palmer's," Rogers replied with a laugh. "And bring Rick."

It was, indeed, business as usual in Washington.

EPILOGUE

Turkmen Whitewash:
The Dream Lives On

MPERSONATING A LOBBYIST HAD BEEN A STRESSFUL EXPERIENCE, and I was hugely relieved when I'd walked out of the offices of Cassidy & Associates back in late February. Still, I had enjoyed the brief period I'd spent as a jet-setting international business agent (even if I was just the flunky of my energy-investing boss) and shaper of global geopolitical affairs.

And it was hard not to daydream about all that I might have accomplished for the "newly elected government of Turkmenistan" if I'd actually had a few million dollars lying around. After all, one dictatorial regime or another is regularly promoted at Washington events similar to the ones that my lobbyist friends had proposed during our discussions.

For example, in May 2006, the government of Uzbek president Islam Karimov staged the U.S. debut of a short video justifying its crackdown a year earlier in the town of Andijan, where security forces killed hundreds of protesters in what Human Rights Watch dubbed a "massacre." The video was shown at a Washington affair at Johns Hopkins University sponsored by the Central Asia–Caucasus Institute (CACI) and co-hosted by CACI director Professor S. Frederick Starr, an adviser on Soviet affairs to Presidents Ronald Reagan and George H. W. Bush. The respected website EurasiaNet.org said Starr "sought to undermine" accounts of Andijan that were critical of the Uzbek government, which had justified the carnage by blaming the demonstration on Islamic militants out to overthrow the government. Independent observers, to the contrary, reported that almost all of the demonstrators were peaceful and unarmed.

It was all in a day's work for Starr, who is perhaps the most outspoken advocate in Washington for the Karimov regime—a regime that once tortured a political prisoner to death with methods that included the use of boiling water and then arrested his elderly mother when she complained. The professor had even penned the fawning preface to the 1998 English-language version of Karimov's page-turner, *Uzbekistan on the Threshold of the Twenty-first Century.* He also speaks fondly of several other despotic governments in central Asia, a region he views almost exclusively through the prism of American geopolitical interests and with little concern for issues such as human rights and corruption.

Starr and his institute are neither intellectually nor financially independent. "Over the years," reads a CACI brochure, "many corporations have provided open-ended support." The corporations named include Chevron, ExxonMobil, and Unocal, as well as Newmont Mining, a company that is deeply entangled with the Karimov regime in Uzbekistan. According to the brochure, CACI's big donors include the Smith Richardson

Foundation and the Bradley Foundation, both extremely conservative institutions that have funded other pro–Caspian regime think tanks. The State Department, the Joint Chiefs of Staff, the National Security Agency, and the Defense Intelligence Agency all have "supported research by CACI scholars," states the brochure, and CACI "benefits from its close contacts with the Washington embassies of the various countries in the region."

In December 2006, the U.S.-Azerbaijan Chamber of Commerce, which promotes Ilham Aliyev's regime courtesy of funding from American oil giants, rolled out the red carpet at a dinner and private reception for first lady and parliament member Mehriban Aliyeva. The first lady, who was presented with the "Goodwill Ambassador Award," has an impressive résumé. Her humanitarian achievements, according to her website, include "inauguration of new objects in Azizbayov district of Baku," visiting "the people damaged during the accident took place at 'Baki Soveti' metro station," and officiating at the "solemn opening of the Baby House 1." On the international front, she has visited Rome and toured the Colosseum.

The reception for the first lady was held just a month after Aliyev's government shut down ANS, Azerbaijan's first private radio and television company, which carried shows produced by the Voice of America and Radio Free Europe/Radio Liberty. "Freedom of the press has virtually disappeared as journalists are being arrested, beaten and intimidated," Congresswoman Janice Schakowsky of Illinois said of the situation in Azerbaijan. "The issue of political prisoners is worsening as more and more people are being detained on politically motivated grounds."

This didn't stop hundreds of people from showing up at the gala, including numerous officials from the State Department, the Pentagon, the National Security Council, and other government agencies. The guests, according to a person in attendance, were served a variety of fine wines, an assortment of appetizers that included lamb tenderloin on grilled focaccia and buckwheat blinis topped with caviar and crème fraîche, and, for their entrée, a choice of cumin-rubbed beef tenderloin or salmon fillet with a pomegranate glaze. For entertainment, there was live music and a dance troupe from Azerbaijan, and each guest was offered a goodie bag stuffed with a small carpet, a photo album about Azerbaijan, and other jazzy bric-a-brac. "I go to a lot of these sorts of things," said my source. "I haven't seen a more lavish affair since the dot-com boom."

The regime of Colonel Muammar Qaddafi, whom Ronald Reagan once described as "the mad dog of the Middle East," came in from the cold under President Bush. In February 2007, the oil-industry-backed U.S.-Libya Business Association brought together government officials from both countries at a gala dinner, held at Charlie Palmer Steak, to honor a senior official of "the Great Socialist People's Libyan Arab Jamahiriya."

Why did Berdymukhamedov deserve less?

To gain a fuller measure of what a little lobbying firepower could have bought Berdymukhamedov and his Stalinist cohort, I attended an all-day conference in 2007 called "Angola Day." The sponsors included the Woodrow Wilson International Center for Scholars, which hosted the event at its downtown headquarters; the Angolan government; and the U.S.-Angola Chamber of Commerce. The latter receives financial support from American oil companies, and its members include numerous former U.S. government officials, including several who have lobbied for Angola. Other than the unfortunate title of the event—had APCO been running the show, it surely would have been less obviously advertorial, perhaps along the lines of "Africa and American Energy Security: Partners in Prosperity"—Angola Day was straight out of the playbook laid out by the Maldon Group's would-be lobbyists: there was the imprimatur of a respected third party—the Wilson Center—a coalition of corporate allies, and a smattering of pliant academics who one day might be willing to write a friendly op-ed about the regime of President Eduardo dos Santos. His government is not as brutal as the one in Turkmenistan, but it surely ranks as one of the most crooked and predatory in the world.

After gaining independence from Portugal in 1975, Angola declared itself a Marxist state and allied itself with the Soviet Union. The CIA supported an insurgency by rebels known as UNITA until the early 1990s, when Angola embraced capitalism following the collapse of the Soviet Union. Dos Santos, who had ruled since 1979, swiftly ditched the military uniform he sometimes wore and began sporting finely tailored suits. The civil war, which left an estimated one million people dead, ended only after rebel leader Jonas Savimbi (embodied by Dolph Lundgren years earlier in the Abramoff-sponsored flick) was killed in combat in 2002.

Angola is sub-Saharan Africa's second largest oil producer after Nigeria, with oil accounting for about 90 percent of its export earnings. Chevron produces about two-thirds of the daily output of oil, a good chunk of which is sold to the United States. Despite billions of dollars in oil revenue, the country ranks 164th among 175 nations on a United Nations index that measures citizens' quality of life. About 80 percent of the population lives in poverty.

It's not hard to unravel this apparent paradox. About $4.2 billion—more than the $3.6 billion the government spent on social programs—disappeared from the Angolan treasury from 1997 through 2002, according to a leaked report by the International Monetary Fund. It said Angola filtered its oil revenue through "a web of opaque offshore accounts." Meanwhile, a stream of investigations has pointed to massive corruption on the part of Dos Santos and other Angolan officials. A Swiss probe identified millions of dollars in bank accounts that allegedly were used by a foreign businessman to pay off Angolan officials. Related investigations by Swiss and French authorities uncovered two private accounts held by Dos Santos in Luxembourg and the Cayman Islands. Global Witness issued a report in 2005 that alleged that Dos Santos's offshore accounts held tens of millions of dollars, including funds diverted from the state treasury.

Angola Day began at 9 A.M. with introductory remarks from speakers representing the sponsors, who were seated at a table atop a stage at the front of a small auditorium. First up was the head of the Wilson Center's Africa Program, former congressman Howard Wolpe. He described the Wilson Center, which was established by Congress in 1968, as a "neutral, nonpartisan institution" that worked to promote fair and open debate. That description didn't quite jibe with the day's scheduled panels, which were stacked with Angolan and American government officials, and a few Beltway bandits whose livelihood depends on their close ties to the Dos Santos regime.

Wolpe was followed by Paul Hare, head of the U.S.-Angola Chamber, who said that the day's events "would not have been possible without the generous support of Angolan and American companies," who were divided into Gold Level sponsors (such as British Petroleum, Chevron, and ExxonMobil), Silver Level (including the U.S.-Africa Energy Association), and Bronze Level (among which was Boeing—a fairly cheap gesture on its part, given that the company had recently sold Angola's national airline six planes). So much for neutrality.

The keynote speaker at the conference was Joaquim David, Angola's elegantly dressed minister of industry, a master at tossing out the full retinue of empty slogans and catchwords that Western audiences hold so dear (and in perfect English as well). David spoke earnestly of his government's commitment to sustainable development, environmental protection, transparency, and social justice—no matter that Dos Santos has demonstrated no interest in such matters since taking power decades ago. The conference had been going on for less than half an hour, but as David rattled off a long list of statistics about economic growth, inflation, and currency rates, audience members were already shifting in their seats, and a few looked to be fighting off slumber.

New life was soon breathed into the proceedings, however: it was time for a coffee break. The crowd of about a hundred bolted for a reception area outside the auditorium, where bountiful platters of pastry and fruits had been laid out, as well as a table topped with silver urns of coffee and stacks of black mugs. It was during this (and subsequent) breaks that the real business of the conference was conducted: political networking, corporate shoptalk, and fawning over the Angolan officials on hand.

There was the remarkably unctuous Witney Schneidman, a former State Department official and member of the chamber, who approached every Angolan official he saw with an ear-to-ear grin on his face; Hank Cohen, a former assistant secretary of state and onetime lobbyist for Angola, chatting up the diamond magnate Maurice Tempelsman; and a Chevron executive and official from the Agency for International Development greeting each other like long-lost friends. As the conference proceedings were about to resume, Derek Campbell of Accession International, which opens doors for corporations seeking business in Africa, handed me his card. "We're sponsoring a cocktail at the Angolan embassy tomorrow night," he told me. "I'd love to have you there."

Cynthia Efird, the American ambassador to Angola moderated a morning panel on "Current Developments in Angola." She complained about media coverage and academic writing on the country, which she said was "stuck in a time warp" that goes back to Angola's civil war, which came to a close in 2002. The "main weapon against this ignorance," she said, was to study the works of scholars such as Schneidman, Hank Cohen, and "our friend" Gerald Bender, a University of Southern California professor who, like Schneidman and Cohen, is a member of the chamber.

A few speakers offered mild criticisms of the Angolan government, among them Deputy Assistant Secretary of State for Democracy, Human Rights, and Labor Jeffrey Krilla, who sported the chamber's pin of the American and Angolan flags on his jacket lapel. Krilla chastised the government for having recently arrested Sarah Wykes, an activist for Global Witness who was freed after a week in jail, and called for greater transparency in managing oil revenues. But his remarks caused no discomfort, especially as he peppered them with conciliatory statements, saying at one point that the State Department applauded Angola for taking "key steps" toward political reform. This was a fairly astonishing comment to make about a government that has ruled for a quarter-century and has repeatedly promised but then postponed the holding of presidential elections (now tentatively set for 2009).

The big-name speaker at Angola Day was Assistant Secretary of State for African Affairs Jendayi Frazer, who addressed the crowd during a luncheon in a neighboring banquet room. As guests munched on shrimp cocktail appetizers and an entrée of roasted duck with lingonberry sauce, Frazer, a chunky woman wearing an African-style dress and a string of pearls, tossed out the same bland bromides as Minister David. "I see Angola as a real model for . . . post-conflict democratic transition," she said from the dais. "Today, we are celebrating real progress in Angola."

Angola Day continued until nightfall, but I bailed out before the closing remarks by Congressman Donald Payne, chairman of the House Subcommittee on Africa and Global Health, and the evening reception, which included another lavish meal and entertainment by an Angolan dance troupe. From the perspective of a consultant for the Maldon Group, this had been a day of glorious possibilities. From my standpoint as an ordinary citizen, it was impossible to stomach any more blather and whitewash.

It was a vision of just how regimes like Angola and Azerbaijan, Nigeria and Equatorial Guinea—the type of serial abrogators of "human dignity" that Condoleezza Rice had so vigorously denounced that spring upon publication of the government's human rights report—can make and keep their wealthy American friends. Someday soon, perhaps, the same will happen for Turkmenistan—God and lobbyists willing.

ACKNOWLEDGMENTS

This book grew out of a story for *Harper's* magazine, so thanks first to a number of people there, especially Bill Wasik for his (standard) brilliant editing, as well as (alphabetically) Paul Ford, Roger Hodge, Rafil Kroll-Zaidi, and John MacArthur.

Thanks also to my agent, Melanie Jackson, and to Bruce Tracy, my editor at Random House.

A number of people advised or otherwise helped me during the writing and editing of this book, the great majority whom prefer to remain anonymous. To those I can name, thanks to Ricardo and Irene, Scott Horton, and Joni Silverstein.

ABOUT THE AUTHOR

KEN SILVERSTEIN is the author of *The Radioactive Boy Scout*. The Washington editor of *Harper's* magazine, he is a former investigative reporter for the Washington, D.C., bureau of the *Los Angeles Times*. Silverstein has also written for *Mother Jones, The Nation,* and *The American Prospect,* among other publications. He lives in Washington.